PHAEDRUS

PLATO stands, with his teacher Socrates and his pupil Aristotle, as one of the shapers of the entire intellectual tradition of the West. Born *c.* 427 BC, he came from a family that had long played a prominent part in Athenian politics, and it would have been natural for him to follow the same course; the reason for his not doing so, according to the seventh of the collection of letters attributed to him (all of them almost certainly inauthentic), was his disillusionment with the kind of politics that could lead, among other things, to the execution – in 399 – of Socrates. Rather less plausibly, the same letter suggests that Plato's several visits to the court of Dionysius II, tyrant of Syracuse in Sicily, were motivated by a desire to put his political theories – as developed above all in his masterwork, *Republic* – into practice. The reform of society on an ethical basis certainly remained one of his central theoretical concerns. However, the focus of his thinking was on ethics itself, in which he first followed and then went beyond Socrates, and on metaphysics and the understanding of reality. In the mid-380s, in Athens, he founded the Academy, the first permanent institution devoted to philosophical research and teaching, and an institution to which all Western universities like to trace their origins.

Plato wrote more than twenty philosophical dialogues, appearing in none himself (most have Socrates as chief speaker). His activity as a writer seems to have lasted over half a century; few authors in any language could claim to rival his particular combination of brilliant artistry and intellectual power. He died in 347 BC.

CHRISTOPHER ROWE is Professor of Greek in the University of Durham, and from 1999 until 2004 held a Leverhulme Personal Research Professorship. Until 1995 he was H. O. Wills Professor of Greek in the University of Bristol, and he has served at various times as President of the International Plato Society, Chair of the Council of University Classical Departments, Chair of the Council of the Classical Association, President of the Society for the Promotion of Hellenic Studies and joint editor of *Phronesis: A Journal for Ancient Philosophy* (Leiden). His books include *Plato* (second edition, 2003), *Reading the Statesman* (edited volume, 1995), *The Cambridge History of Greek and Roman Thought* (edited with Malcolm Schofield, 2000) and *New Perspectives on Plato, Modern and Ancient* (edited with Julia Annas, 2002). In Sarah Broadie and Christopher Rowe, *Aristotle, Nicomachean Ethics* (2002), Sarah Broadie's philosophical commentary is accompanied by his translation. He has also translated, and/or written commentaries on, Plato's *Phaedrus* (1986), *Phaedo* (1993), *Statesman* (1995) and *Symposium* (1998) and, with Terry Penner, has written a monograph on the *Lysis*. His present project is a comprehensive treatment of Plato's strategies as a writer of philosophy.

PLATO

Phaedrus

Translated with an Introduction and Notes by
CHRISTOPHER ROWE

PENGUIN BOOKS

PENGUIN CLASSICS

Published by the Penguin Group
Penguin Books Ltd, 80 Strand, London WC2R ORL, England
Penguin Group (USA) Inc., 375 Hudson Street, New York, New York 10014, USA
Penguin Group (Canada), 10 Alcorn Avenue, Toronto, Ontario, Canada M4V 3B2
(a division of Pearson Penguin Canada Inc.)
Penguin Ireland, 25 St Stephen's Green, Dublin 2, Ireland
(a division of Penguin Books Ltd)
Penguin Group (Australia), 250 Camberwell Road,
Camberwell, Victoria 3124, Australia (a division of Pearson Australia Group Pty Ltd)
Penguin Books India Pvt Ltd, 11 Community Centre,
Panchsheel Park, New Delhi – 110 017, India
Penguin Group (NZ), cnr Airborne and Rosedale Roads, Albany,
Auckland 1310, New Zealand (a division of Pearson New Zealand Ltd)
Penguin Books (South Africa) (Pty) Ltd, 24 Sturdee Avenue,
Rosebank 2196, South Africa

Penguin Books Ltd, Registered Offices: 80 Strand, London WC2R ORL, England

www.penguin.com

This translation first published in 2005

10

Introduction and Further Reading © Christopher Rowe, 2005

Set in 10.25/12.25 pt PostScript Adobe Sabon
Typeset by Rowland Phototypesetting Ltd, Bury St Edmunds, Suffolk
Printed in Great Britain by Clays Ltd, St Ives plc

ISBN-13: 978-0-140-44974-7

www.greenpenguin.co.uk

Contents

Acknowledgements

I offer thanks to Adrian and Lucinda Phillips (of Aris & Phillips), who first invited me to tackle the *Phaedrus*, and who published the volume that is the direct ancestor of the present one (*Plato: Phaedrus*, 1986; second edition, 2000); to David Brown of Oxbow Books, who as the new owner of the Aris & Phillips imprint gave permission for me to reuse my translation (though in the event I have significantly modified it) and scattered material from the commentary; to David Hopkins, who was largely responsible for the translation of a number of short verse passages Plato includes in his text; to the Leverhulme Trust, without whose grant to me of a Personal Research Professorship this second journey of mine through the *Phaedrus* would not have been possible; to Terry Penner, in whose company my appreciation of Plato's philosophical acuity and literary sophistication continues to develop; to my wife Heather, for perpetual support (and tolerance) and for reading the proofs; and to Laura Barber, for proposing to me the project of a new Penguin *Phaedrus*.

CHRISTOPHER ROWE
June 2004

Chronology

We know as little about Plato's life as we do about most of his peers. Plato is chiefly known as a writer, of course, but what passed for 'publication' in ancient Athens was so far removed from the modern world that it is hard to say even that a dialogue was published around such-and-such a year. The relative dating of the dialogues is often controversial too, and many scholars nowadays prefer to study each dialogue on its own, rather than as part of a corpus. The situation is confused by the presence of a number of works which are spurious or at least of uncertain authorship: they have been omitted below. Nevertheless, study of Plato's writing style has resulted in a broad division of the dialogues into three groups, which is reflected in the (very rough) chronology below. For this division, see especially Charles Kahn, 'On Platonic Chronology', in Julia Annas and Christopher Rowe (eds), *New Perspectives on Plato, Ancient and Modern*) Cambridge, MA: Harvard University Press, 2002), pp. 93–127.

c. 427 BC Birth of Plato, son of Ariston, in Athens into a well-connected and noble family. The story that the name 'Plato' derived from the adjective *platus*, 'broad' (referring to the width of the great man's shoulders; or his intellectual capacity; or the 'breadth' of his style) has been discredited.

418–416 Dramatic date for the dialogue between Socrates and Phaedrus.

404 The defeat of Athens in the Peloponnesian War (which started in 431) signals the temporary end of the democracy which had governed Athens for most of the last hundred

years. It is replaced by a cruel junta of oligarchs, at least
two of whom are members of Plato's immediate family. The
Thirty Tyrants, as they become known, last only a few
months before being overthrown in a civil war and replaced
by a revived democracy.

399 The new democratic government puts Socrates, Plato's
mentor for the past few years, on trial. The charges are:
failing to recognize the gods recognized by the State, but
introducing new deities, and corrupting the young. Socrates'
condemnation and subsequent execution by drinking hem-
lock are the last straw: Plato more or less withdraws from
the world of practical politics.

390s Plato and other disciples find it expedient to leave Athens
for a while and stay in nearby Megara. Plato may also have
travelled around the eastern Mediterranean. Meanwhile, he
is beginning to write.

390s–380s Plato composes a large and varied group of dialogues:
Defence of Socrates ('*Apology*'), *Charmides*, *Cratylus*, *Crito*,
Euthydemus, *Euthyphro*, *Gorgias*, *Hippias Minor*, *Ion*,
Laches, *Lysis*, *Menexenus*, *Meno*, *Phaedo*, *Protagoras*,
Symposium.

389–388 Plato visits Sicily and southern Italy and establishes
contact with the Pythagorean schools there.

c. 387 Plato founds the Academy, a research institute, adjacent
to one of the main gymnasia of Athens, a little to the north-
west of the ancient city, which was sacred to the local hero
Academus.

380s–370s Second group of dialogues: *Parmenides*, *Phaedrus*,
Republic, *Theaetetus*.

367 Second visit to Sicily, at the invitation of Dion, uncle
of Dionysius II, tyrant of Syracuse. Some have supposed
that Plato had hopes of making Dionysius an ideal ruler, a
philosopher-king; if so, they were soon dashed. Plato
evidently had some difficulty getting home.

c. 365 Arrival in the Academy of its most eminent student,
Aristotle.

361 Plato visits Sicily once more, for unknown reasons; in any
case this visit too seems to have ended badly.

360s–350s Third group of dialogues: *Philebus, Sophist, States-man, Timaeus-Critias, Laws* (known to be Plato's last work; he may have been still working on it when he died).
347 Plato dies.

Introduction

At the beginning of the *Phaedrus*,[1] the philosopher Socrates meets Phaedrus,[2] an amateur rhetorical enthusiast passionately devoted to professional displays, and the conversation between the two of them lasts for the whole of the work. If the dramatic date of the dialogue is somewhere around 418–416 BC,[3] Socrates is in his fifties (he was born in 469), Phaedrus in his mid-twenties; despite the claims of some scholars, there is no evidence in the work of anything beyond friendship between them. This is a point that needs making, for the Socrates of Plato's dialogues is usually represented as someone with a keen interest in beautiful young men or boys (though as he says in the *Charmides*, 'pretty well all of them, at the right age, appear beautiful to me' (154b9–10) – and he then goes on to say, typically, that he won't know whether anyone is really beautiful until he knows the state of his *soul*). Moreover, one of the chief topics of the dialogue is *erôs* – i.e. passionate or (as it would normally be understood) romantic love. So it would not have been in the least surprising if the *Phaedrus* had involved some sort of erotic by-play, perhaps the suggestion of an erotic relationship, between its characters, making the action of the dialogue – as so often in Plato – mirror its content. The *Symposium*, in many ways the companion dialogue of the *Phaedrus*, is full of such by-play, while the *Lysis*, a third, shorter and more puzzling treatment of love, starts and ends with Hippothales' passion for Lysis. In the *Phaedrus*, by contrast, the characters – Socrates and Phaedrus – are content merely to *talk* about love, and lovers, as observers.

For in fact, both Phaedrus and Socrates have other kinds

of love, other kinds of obsession. They are both mad about
logoi, the most general meaning of which would be 'words', or
'things said'. But the two men are mad about rather different
kinds of 'things said': in Phaedrus' case, it is *speeches*, whereas
for Socrates it is *talk* and, as it will turn out, 'talk' of a rather
special (philosophical) kind. When the pair of them meet,
Phaedrus is fresh from hearing a rhetorical performance by his
'darling' Lysias, someone of about the same age as himself[4] but
evidently already making his mark as an orator. This speech
was a display on a paradoxical theme: an imaginary appeal by
a man to an adolescent boy to grant him sexual favours, but
with the novelty that the man in question is (so he pretends, at
any rate) not in love with the boy. Socrates proceeds to tease
Phaedrus about his feigned reluctance to rehearse the speech
to him:

Phaedrus – if I don't know Phaedrus, I've forgotten even who I am.
But I do, and I haven't; I know perfectly well that when he heard
Lysias' speech he did not hear it just once but repeatedly asked him to
go through it for him, and Lysias responded readily. But for Phaedrus
not even that was enough, and in the end he borrowed the book and
examined the things in it which he was most eager to look at, and
doing this he sat from sun-up until he was tired and went for a walk,
as *I* think – I'll swear by the Dog it's true – knowing the speech quite
off by heart, unless it was a rather long one. He was going outside the
wall to practise it, when he met the very person who is sick with
passion for hearing people speak – and 'seeing, seeing him', he was
glad, because he would have a companion in his manic frenzy, and he
told him to lead on. Then when the one in love with speeches asked
him to speak, he put on a pose, as if not eager to speak; but in the
end, even if no one wanted to listen, he meant to use force, and *would*
speak. So you, Phaedrus, you just ask him to do here and now what
he will soon do anyway. (228a5–c5)

Right from the beginning, then, we know something about
where the two men's passions lie. At this stage, Socrates makes
out that it is Phaedrus' kind of *logoi* that he is 'sick with passion'
about; he discovers that Phaedrus actually has the written ver-

sion of the speech hidden on his person and eventually makes him read it out. (The speech just might be a genuine product of Lysias' but is more likely to be an imitation by Plato himself. It contains just the sorts of things Lysias would have said, piling point upon point in the way he did – for the lawcourts.)

But Lysias' speech does not impress Socrates, and he goes on to give a rival speech, on the same subject, of his own – or rather, as he claims, not of his own: he must have got it from someone or somewhere else,[5] because he knows nothing at all about speech-making, or about the subject. He is still concerned – so he suggests – about putting on a poor showing in front of Phaedrus, and so he gives the speech with his head covered, allegedly to prevent his feeling ashamed as he sees Phaedrus' reactions (237a). However, he has hardly finished when it suddenly emerges that he has a much more important reason to be ashamed: it was just a 'dreadful' speech, 'foolish and somewhat impious' (242d4, 7), because of what it said about – that is, against – love. There follows the famous 'palinode', or speech of repentance, which praises love, and the god of love, as the greatest of good things, and describes the winged soul traversing the cosmos: a speech of extraordinary range and virtuosity that has always been, for ancient as well as modern readers, the main focus of interest in the *Phaedrus*. What Socrates offers us in this new, second, speech – so he gives us to understand – is more like the truth of the matter: love may be a form of madness, as Lysias had originally claimed (who would prefer to deal with a mad person when he could deal with a sane one?), but when it comes from the gods, madness is actually preferable to sanity.

How so? Because the madness that Socrates has in mind is the madness of *philosophia*, the 'love of wisdom'. And in the picture he gives of the ideal pair of lover and beloved, we have a glimpse of what he means by calling himself 'sick with passion for hearing people speak'; for what this ideal pair does is to talk, as their means of access to, or (in terms of the special theory to which Socrates refers) as the recovery of, the knowledge or wisdom they both desire.

After Socrates'[6] second speech, he initiates a long discussion of what it is for a *logos* ('speech', 'talk', 'discussion', 'discourse' or just 'thing said') to be a good or a bad one, and then of what one's attitude should be towards one's verbal 'offspring', whether written or spoken. Fundamentally, the conclusions are that what distinguishes a good speech from a bad one is whether or not it is based on knowledge (and also whether it is framed appropriately for its audience); and that one should never be too attached to what one has written, or said, because one should always be able to *improve* on it – something which itself seems to be an essential feature of philosophical dialogue (conversation) as Socrates understands it. So the dialogue ends as it began, on the subject of *logoi*; but now we have moved a world away from the supposedly virtuosic displays of speakers like Lysias, in which truth plays no role, to 'talk' of a quite different kind. Accordingly, in the dying moments of their conversation, Socrates instructs Phaedrus to convey their second main conclusion, about a speaker's proper attitude towards his speeches, to Lysias (now merely Phaedrus' *friend*, no longer his 'darling') (278e4). Phaedrus retorts by suggesting that Socrates do the same to *his* friend Isocrates, thus showing how little he has learned. As Socrates shows by his response, it is rather their *other* conclusion that should be reported to Isocrates, about the importance, for the expert orator, of knowledge. In short, Socrates hopes that Isocrates will become a philosopher. In fact, though Isocrates was to become[7] one of the most outstanding and influential intellectual figures of the fourth century BC, he did so in part in direct and open opposition to Plato, constructing his own, rival, notion of what it was to do 'philosophy'. While Lysias may have been an outstanding courtroom orator, Isocrates pioneered a whole system of education – but through rhetoric; neither in his voluminous writings nor in his speaking did he live up to what Socrates claims to hope for him.

This will give a sense of the general structure of the dialogue. What it illustrates is a typical Platonic strategy: that of starting – or rather, of having Socrates start – by giving the appearance of sharing the very premises that he means to question, and then, little by little, clarifying the terms of the argument so that, finally, we understand just what it was that Socrates was really saying at the beginning (though many readers will already have had their suspicions). Thus Socrates *appears*, at the beginning of the conversation with Phaedrus, to share exactly Phaedrus' own interests; that, at any rate, is how Phaedrus understands it, and, as I have already suggested, he probably still half thinks the same thing at the end. But the reader is left in no doubt that Socrates' passion is not for *speeches* at all.

So in that case, one may reasonably ask, what on earth is he doing when he gives not just one but two speeches, together taking up a fair proportion of the whole of the *Phaedrus*? No reader is going to be fooled by Socrates' repeated denials that they are his own speeches, especially when he frequently appears in other dialogues as sponsoring ideas that are either very like or identical to many of those that he, or whoever it is that is supposedly inspiring him, offers us in the second speech. It could perhaps be that the *Phaedrus* marks his (or rather Plato's) *repudiation* of those ideas:[8] what will be substituted, from now on, for all that talk about the soul's encounter with True Reality, beyond the heavens, is some businesslike, down-to-earth application of proper philosophical method, and hard analysis. To that one might raise the objection that, later on in the conversation with Phaedrus, Socrates will use both his speeches as themselves *examples* of expert *logos*-making; in particular, he will praise them for starting with a definition of their subject (*erôs*) in a way that Lysias' speech did not (263d–265c). What is more, he will by implication identify the method they used with the very philosophical method[9] that, he will say, is a *sine qua non* for the truly expert speaker/writer. However, given that Plato places such importance on the speaker's knowing the truth, he cannot in any case want to write off Socrates' speeches as actually false:[10] they are, at worst, a brilliantly suggestive story about the nature and fate of the soul, its desires and aspirations. Part of Socrates' own verdict on his second speech goes like this:

   . . . the madness of love we said was best, and by expressing the experience of love through some kind of simile, which allowed us perhaps to grasp some truth, though maybe also it took us in a wrong direction, and mixing together a not wholly implausible speech, we sang a playful hymn in the form of a story ... (265b5–c1)

So perhaps the message is: Even though it was all well done, we shouldn't take it too seriously (for I, Socrates/Plato, don't).[11] Socrates gives no indication as to what he got right and where he went off (maybe) in a wrong direction; but his general message is that we always need to move on and should never be content to be identified with anything we have written (279b–d). We may even take the end of the *Phaedrus* as expressing Plato's view on his own written products.[12] Indeed it is hard, though many have tried,[13] not to take it this way, so insistent does Socrates appear to be on applying his conclusion about the value of speech-making and speech-writing to *every* genre of writing.

If that is the case, however, it will also be hard to suppose that he means to be disowning any particular ideas in the speech. What the argument of the *Phaedrus* is here pointing to is perhaps just the danger of relying on any medium that does not allow for questioning, challenge and the prospect of progress to a better understanding. Socrates' description of his own performance, that it 'allowed us perhaps to grasp some truth, though maybe also it took us in a wrong direction', will in that case apply to any *logos*, if taken just by itself; and it will apply even to the *best* kind – which, I myself propose, the combination of Socrates' two speeches in the *Phaedrus* is ultimately designed to exemplify. 'If you are going to make speeches, do it this way,' Plato will be saying ('but always beware of taking your products too seriously; the truth is too important for that'). And as a matter of fact, the Socrates of the *Phaedrus* seems to be committed to saying that there will be occasions for speech-making; for how else are we to take his proposals for a reformed rhetoric, based on truth and adapted to the specific nature of the audience?

Since the power of speech is in fact a leading of the soul, the man who means to be an expert in rhetoric must know how many forms soul has. Thus their number is so and so, and they are of such and such kinds, which is why some people are like this, and others like that; and these having been distinguished in this way, then again there are so many forms of speeches, each one of such and such a kind. People of one kind are easily persuaded for one sort of reason by one kind of speech to hold one kind of opinion, while people of another kind are for some other sorts of reasons difficult to persuade.

Having then grasped these things satisfactorily, after that the student must observe them as they are in real life, and actually being put into practice, and be able to follow them with keen perception, or otherwise be as yet no further on from the things he heard earlier when he was with me. But when he both has sufficient ability to say what sort of man is persuaded by what sorts of things, and is capable of telling himself when he observes him that *this* is the man, *this* the nature of person that was discussed before, now actually present in front of him, to whom he must now apply *these* kinds of speech in *this* way in order to persuade him of *this* kind of thing; when he now has all of this, and has also grasped the occasions for speaking and for holding back, and again for speaking concisely and piteously and in an exaggerated fashion, and for all the forms of speeches he may learn, recognizing the right and the wrong time for these, *then* his grasp of the science will be well and completely finished, but not before that; but in whichever of these things someone is lacking when he speaks or teaches or writes, and says that he speaks scientifically, the person who disbelieves him is in the stronger position. (Socrates at 271c10–272b2; put in the mouth of an imagined writer of the ideal rhetoric textbook)

Fitting what he says to the nature of his hearers: this might not be a natural role for Socrates himself, who is happiest (so he might claim) telling things straight.[14] Yet here, on this occasion, with Phaedrus, circumstances contrive to make him take the role on, and – as he says – his speech is 'forced to use somewhat poetical language *because of Phaedrus*': is that, in part, because he thinks that kind of language appropriate to the nature of Phaedrus' soul?[15] The subsequent discussion certainly shows Phaedrus to be less than the ideal recipient for straight (philosophical) talking.[16]

Thus, on the account I myself prefer, Socrates' second speech is a statement of things that he is – in some form or other – supposed to believe, even if he will stake nothing on it.[17] This will help to explain its sheer *length*: among other things, it gives us a sketch of the kind of view of the whole – the 'babbling and lofty talk about nature' (270a1) that Socrates will propose as a requirement of any science. In that sense, it will do no harm to treat the speech as a kind of compendium of Platonic ideas, a role to which it is, up to a point, ideally suited. There are, however, two dangers about this. The first, which by now speaks for itself, is that it will have become detached from the warnings Plato has so carefully attached to it: '*only* a sketch'; 'no detail to be pressed'; 'right in a way, perhaps, but maybe also misleading'.[18] It will then suffer the fate that Socrates predicts for all written documents:

. . . when once it is written, every composition trundles about every-where in the same way, in the presence both of those who know about the subject and of those who have nothing at all to do with it, and it does not know how to address those it should address and not those it should not. When it is ill treated and unjustly abused, it always needs its father to help it; for it is incapable of either defending or helping itself. (275d9–e5)

'Ill treatment' or 'abuse', in this case, will be a matter of treating the speech as an account of Platonic *doctrine* (an approach that would misrepresent Plato himself, not just the palinode of the *Phaedrus*: Plato no doubt has plenty of firmly held convictions, but he is perfectly serious – as any reading across his dialogues will show – about wanting in every case to leave room for re-statement and, in general, for progress). But there is also a second danger involved in lifting Socrates' second speech from its context in the *Phaedrus* as a whole. This is that we are likely to forget, or play down, two facts about it: firstly, that it is intended also, and in the first place, as an account of love (*erôs*), in response to Lysias' own; secondly, and more importantly, that we are likely to miss that this account of Socrates', in responding to Lysias', is full of deliberate *paradox*. Lysias set out to dazzle by taking on an absurd and even self-contradictory thesis; Socrates out-dazzles him, first by treating the philosopher, that exemplar (surely) of rationality, as *mad*, then – even more extraordinarily – by giving Phaedrus, and us, an ideal *erôs* that seems to overturn the whole idea of *erôs*. (*Erôs* without sex? What on earth next? Isn't sex what *erôs* is ultimately about?)

There is, however, a difference between Lysianic paradox and Socratic paradox. Lysianic paradox merely allows Lysias to appear clever. Socratic paradoxes, by contrast, even while being *para doxan* (literally 'contrary to belief' – i.e. contrary to all our expectations), are things Socrates actually believes are *true*.[19] That is, they give us ways of seeing how the world actually is, without excluding the possibility of other, complementary, ways of seeing it. So the philosopher *is* crazy, not because most people think he is (on the superficial grounds that he is not interested in the things that interest them), but because he obsesses about truth with the same intensity that an ordinary lover obsesses about his darling. And ideal *erôs must* be without sex, if it is – ideally – a passion for Beauty (as the speech suggests), not for the bit of beauty that happens to be present in this particular body (and soul), since sex with this body will merely distract from the search for Beauty, about which the ideal beloved will be equally obsessive.[20]

We may, if we like, call this a kind of appropriation. But it can also be seen as part of that Platonic strategy I described earlier: appearing to start where others are, when actually, all the time, being somewhere else. Just as Socrates seemed, at any rate to Phaedrus, to be sharing Phaedrus' enthusiasm for speech-making while actually being focused on something else, so he gives his first speech as if wholly endorsing Lysias' view of *erôs* as culpable madness, and as being concerned solely with sexual fulfilment. But when we reach his later assessment of his two speeches, we find that he was not actually doing that at all, for the first speech was, all along, just a description of one part of *erôs* and one part of madness. It is not that he has changed his mind about that first speech: that he speaks with his head covered shows that he *already* knows what he is doing – i.e. preparing to give a one-sided ('impious') account of *erôs*, as if that were the whole of it.[21] For him, the lover is actually mad, only not – if he's the ideal lover – in the way Lysias thinks; and the lover is actually obsessed with sexual fulfilment, but only if he's a non-ideal lover.[22]

There is another extended example of the same phenomenon[23] in the second speech. Towards the end, Socrates embarks on a vivid description of the sprouting of feathers all over the surface of the soul of the ideal lover, as he observes his beautiful beloved, and remembers – or half-remembers – Beauty Itself, which he once glimpsed, at some divine feast in the heavens . . .[24] This passage (250c–252c) is the most deliberately *erotic* in the whole dialogue, evoking at every step ordinary – male – sexual excitement, from the first stirrings of arousal through to ejaculation, along with the behaviour of the ordinary, common-or-garden lover. Now this is, to be sure, in part a kind of playfulness. But it also has a serious point: it is not merely the case (so I suggest Plato is saying) that there is a general kind of parallel between erotic passion and the love of wisdom, but that the actual experience of encountering some aspect, some dimly realized part of the truth in the company of someone else,[25] is just like that; it makes one's *hair stand on end*, as we might put it, only Plato chooses to put it more graphically. 'Intercourse' with the objects of knowledge, in other words, is no *mere* metaphor, metaphor though it still is. In this way he makes the strong claim that in denying himself ordinary sexual gratification, the philosopher actually denies himself nothing, for when it comes to it he will get something that is the same, only better. It is not so much that *erôs* has been de-sexualised; rather, sex has been injected into philosophy.[26]

Much ink has been spilled[27] on the question of the *unity* of the *Phaedrus*. At one point Socrates expresses his view, and expects Phaedrus to accept, 'that every speech should be put together like a living creature, as it were with a body of its own, so as not to lack either a head or feet, but to have both middle parts and extremities, so written as to fit both each other and the whole' (264c2–5); and yet the *Phaedrus* itself has seemed, to many readers, to have nothing at all organic about it. In particular, the second part of the dialogue (from the end of Socrates' second speech) has seemed insufficiently connected with the first. However, if what I have said in the preceding paragraphs takes us at least broadly in the right direction, the problem largely disappears. True, the second part has nothing directly to say about *erôs*, which appears to be the main subject of the first part; and the second part has little or nothing of the wit and subtlety that adorn the first – again true. But it is no less true to say that the dialogue remains focused throughout on the subject of *logoi* ('speeches', 'speaking', 'talk' and so on), and that *erôs*, as Socrates understands it, is itself all about *logoi* – the 'talk' that leads us to the ultimate object of *erôs* (Beauty or, more generally, knowledge). But this means that the choice facing Phaedrus, and us, is not just between different kinds of talk but between different kinds of *life*.

In other words, the real subject of the *Phaedrus* is pretty much that of the *Symposium* (and also that of the *Lysis*): the nature of human motivation. However, the Socrates of the *Phaedrus* takes a radically different view on this subject from his counterpart in the *Symposium*. In the *Symposium*, there are no irrational parts to the soul: all desire is for the (real) good, and the only difference between individuals has to do with their beliefs about what that good consists in. (Extraordinarily, nowhere in the account of *erôs* that Socrates offers on the authority of the priestess Diotima is there any mention, or even hint, of irrational desire; we are assumed to love good and beautiful things, and to go for whatever we identify as good and beautiful.[28]) In the *Phaedrus*, however, the soul is divided into three parts, as in the *Republic*: one rational (which Socrates compares to the charioteer of a two-horse team) and two irrational (the two horses, a white one on the right, and a black one on the left).

Socrates may even implicitly acknowledge this difference in the *Phaedrus* when he replies to a question Phaedrus asks him about his attitude to the old myths:

. . . I am not yet capable of 'knowing myself', in accordance with the Delphic inscription; so it seems absurd to me that while I am still ignorant of this subject I should inquire into things which do not belong to me. So then saying goodbye to these things, and believing what is commonly thought about them, what I was saying just now, I inquire not into these but into myself, to see whether I am actually a beast more complex [i.e divided?] and more typhonic than Typhon, or both a tamer and a simpler [i.e. unified, rational?] creature, sharing some divine and un-Typhonic portion by nature. (229e6–230a6)

However, to see this as a reference to the two alternative models of soul or mind is somewhat speculative,[29] not least because the *Phaedrus* will later distinguish on its own terms between simple and complex souls: (probably) those which are predominantly rational, and those in which 'rule' is uncertainly shared by the different parts (277c (cf. 269d–272b)). What is beyond reasonable doubt, or so I hold, is that the *Symposium* takes seriously the idea that there is only one object of desire – our good, and our happiness – so that there is no room for conflict between desire and reason. (If we go off in different directions, that is not because of our desires but because of our *decisions* about which way to go, based upon our beliefs plus our universal desire for the good.)[30] Meanwhile, beyond *any* doubt, the *Phaedrus* proposes a view of things that makes conflict endemic, at least in any erotic context. Here Socrates recognizes distinct elements in us that naturally tend in different directions: appetite pulls towards immediate pleasure, and excess, while reason pulls away from that towards restraint, under the guidance of reflections about what is best.

This is the schema on which Socrates builds his first speech;[31] in the second, he adds the white horse as the instinctive, but not wholly reliable, ally of the charioteer of reason.[32] It is this radical division of the soul, and its attribution to the soul of more than one object of desire, that (so one supposes) causes souls to be 'complex', or 'variegated' (*poikilos*) (277c2), and makes the new rhetoric – which knows how to persuade different types of soul – so important. Socrates may have preferred to tell things straight; on the *Symposium* model, it also makes sense for him to do so, for on that model we are all essentially rational beings. What we do is determined by our beliefs, and what other way is there of reliably changing our beliefs than trying (rationally) to persuade us? But the presence, or arrival, of the black horse changes everything. In the image, it is only a mixture of force and habituation that will finally calm him down and stop him demanding immediate gratification. This is why even the ideal orator will need to be versatile: to 'grasp the occasions for speaking and for holding back, and again for speaking concisely and piteously and in an exaggerated fashion, and for all the forms of speeches he may learn, recognizing the right and the wrong time for these' (272a4–7). In short, in addition to the truth he will need all those special skills that ordinary orators have.[33] Once again, the topics of 'speech(es)' and love, *logos* and *erôs*, turn out to be vitally connected.

NOTES

1. In order to refer to particular passages in the dialogue, this volume uses – as do all modern translations and editions – the page numbers and page sections (usually five, marked a–e) as fixed by the Stephanus edition of Plato, dating from the Renaissance. (Line numbers vary between different editions of the Greek text; the ones given in this volume are those of Burnet's 1903 Oxford edition.) Thus '227b' in note 3 below means 'section b of page 227 of the relevant Stephanus volume' – as marked in the margin of the translation.

2. The modern reader who hears the name 'Phaedrus' is likely to think of Robert M. Pirsig's excellent *Zen and the Art of Motorcycle Maintenance: An Inquiry into Value* (first published in Britain by The Bodley Head Ltd in 1974). But Pirsig's Phaedrus is rather more of a philosopher than Plato's; see below.

3. I here follow Nails 2003, Appendix 1, abandoning the view that the dialogue has no possible dramatic date. (I endorsed the latter view in 1986, on the basis that Lysias was still living in Thurii in the 410s; but there is no reason why he should not have been visiting Athens, as is actually suggested by the fact that the *Phaedrus* has him staying at Epicrates' house: 227b. The signs in the dialogue generally seem to point to a date not long before 415, when Phaedrus was exiled for his alleged part in the notorious profanation of the Eleusinian mysteries.)

4. And not *literally* his darling (236b); Phaedrus is only interested in Lysias' speeches.

5. From Sappho or Anacreon, or some prose writers (235c)? Or because he is possessed by the nymphs of the place (madness again: 238d, 241e)?

6. Once again Socrates does his best to disclaim responsibility for what he says. And indeed speeches of such length are not his usual style, which is rather question-and-answer, with himself typically in the questioning role – in other words, 'dialogue', or 'conversation' (*dialegesthai*). In the second half of the *Phaedrus* he is himself again (in dialogue).

7. And indeed had become, by the time of writing of the *Phaedrus* (perhaps in the third decade of the fourth century?).

8. This is essentially the view of Nehamas and Woodruff (in the Introduction to the Hackett translation of the *Phaedrus*, 1995).

9. I.e. 'collection and division', which means, roughly, finding the genus under which the thing to be defined falls, then dividing the genus into its species, until one reaches the *definiendum*, the thing to be defined, itself: so *erôs* belongs to the genus madness, but its true nature only emerges (so the second speech makes clear) when one knows what *species* of madness it is.

10. The first *is* initially represented as false – but only insofar as it pretends, and actually pretended (for a moment), to give the whole of what love is. When taken together with the second speech (as in 263–5), the first – so Socrates finally suggests – gives part of the truth.

11. And no reader of the speech is likely to miss the fact that the speech is by turns serious, witty and playful, and sometimes both at once (when irony – always one of Plato's favourite weapons – sets in).

12. Some (one of whom is Szlezák 1999) have seen Plato here as signalling to, or reminding, an inner circle of readers, perhaps in or around the newly founded Platonic Academy, that they needed to go behind the written dialogues, to whatever was in Plato's *oral* teaching. This remains a minority interpretation.

13. E.g. by stressing the un-speech-like character of Plato's dialogues; yet the poets are certainly included, and some of them (the ones who wrote plays) also used dialogue.

14. Cf. *Gorgias* 521d–522a, a famous passage in which he identifies himself as perhaps the only true statesman in existence, precisely on the grounds that he tells people the truth whether they like it or not. The theory of rhetoric in the *Phaedrus* might – though it

need not – be taken as identifying ways of persuading people of the truth *without* upsetting them.

15. In that case, I take it, Phaedrus' will be a 'complex' soul, which requires 'complex speeches containing all the modes' (277c2–3): see further below.

16. Why should Plato portray Socrates faced with so unreceptive and unpromising an interlocutor? The suggestion I find most attractive is one put forward by Jonathan Lear in a session (on, as it happened, Blondell 2002) at the 2004 meeting of the Pacific Division of the American Philosophical Association: namely (if I may so summarize Lear's view) that as we observe Phaedrus' superficial relationship with *logoi* (one which puts him on a par with the 'lovers of sights and sounds' at the end of *Republic* V), we are, as a result, meant to be inoculated against taking a similarly limited view of things ourselves.

17. I.e. because – to be true to his principles, as later enunciated – he would be content to be asked to reconsider (try to improve on) any part of it; and also to the extent that the statement may be specifically formulated *for Phaedrus* (cf. n. 15 above). However, a passage like 271c–272b, cited in the text above ('Since the power of speech is in fact a leading of the soul, the man who means to be an expert in rhetoric must know how many forms soul has', and so on), nowhere suggests that the ideal orator will ever *lie* to his audience.

18. We shall also tend to miss the *wit* in Socrates' performance (see n. 11 above); compendia might be expected to be read po-faced. (As a matter of fact, many modern readers, and probably many ancient ones too, *have* missed this aspect of the speech – a singular loss.)

19. Only up to a point, then, is Socratic paradox itself a matter of play; or perhaps, in the end, it is not play at all.

20. Thus, to spell it out: bizarrely, what the ideal lover is in love with is not actually the one he calls his 'beloved' but something else. The same sort of idea appears both in the *Symposium* and in the *Lysis*; it is not something invented just for the occasion of the *Phaedrus* – that is, if we suppose, as most do, that the *Phaedrus* was written later than at least one of the other two.

21. Of course he has an excuse ready for covering his head: Phaedrus will scoff at his amateurism. (But why should we accept that explanation from someone who has already shown no qualms about expressing firm views on the failings of Lysias' effort?)

22. In Socrates' second speech, even those pairs who *occasionally*

give in to the black horses of appetite (i.e. plain lust) will be disqualified from the prize available to those who never do (256b–e).

23. Or, to put it more carefully, a similar one.

24. The soul's wings/feathers are what will, or may, ultimately carry this soul up, and back, to Beauty.

25. It is not clear whether the experience depends on the presence of someone else; but then Socrates is specifically describing relationships.

26. Much here depends on how we take 252b1–9, which I translate this way: 'This experience, my beautiful boy, the one to whom my speech is addressed, men term love; but when you hear what gods call it I expect you will laugh, because of your youth.' I think some Homeric experts cite two verses to Love from the less well-known poems, the second of which is quite outrageous (*hubristikon*) and not very metrical; they celebrate Love like this: 'We mortals call him Mighty Love, a wingèd power of great renown, / Immortals call him Fledgeling Dove – since Eros' wings lack down.' By contrast, Nehamas and Woodruff 1995 give 'less well known poems, of which the second *is quite indecent* (my italics) and does not scan very well. They praise Love this way: "Yes, mortals call him powerful winged 'Love'; / But because of his need to thrust out his wings, the gods call him 'Shove'" ' – explaining in a footnote that 'the indecency is in the word *pterophutôr* ("wing-thrusting")'. If they are right, Plato will presumably be drawing attention to the 'obscenity' of the preceding description, which the two made-up verses round off; that description will, then (so far as I can see), merely be teasing, even pornographic. However, there is nothing inherently obscene or indecent about *pterophutôr*, which simply means 'wing-sprouting'. Rather, I suggest, Plato teases us by merely *appearing*, momentarily, to be about to bring in something obscene (this with the adjective *hubristikon*: since Socrates' first speech, *hubris* has been specifically associated with lust), and then immediately explaining the 'outrage', or 'excess', as mere metrical 'outrage'.

27. By myself, among others: see Further Reading.

28. Cf. Nehamas and Woodruff 1995, Introduction, p. xxxix. (It seems to me wrong, however, to describe the *Symposium* as saying that '(a)n undivided soul, all of it always desiring *what it considers best*, is subject to no such conflicts [sc. between appetite and reason]': what every soul wants, according to Diotima, is presumably real, not merely apparent, happiness.)

29. As would be the suggestion that it might have been partly this
    change of view that led Plato to write another dialogue about
    erôs, although I am myself content to speculate in that way. (It
    is around here that I finally lose any sympathy with the view,
    still held in one or two quarters, that the *Phaedrus* could have
    been Plato's first dialogue. This proposal stems especially from
    the point that the dialogue is, in a way, or can be seen as,
    programmatic; and shouldn't programmes come before, rather
    than during, the event? However, there are just too many of what
    look like cross-references to other dialogues; not to see them as
    such seems to imply a Plato who, implausibly, began with most
    of his most characteristic ideas already fully formed in his head.

30. See e.g. *Symposium* 205d1–7, with surrounding context.

31. I.e. even before we reach the simile of the charioteer and his
    horses, which dresses up the same ideas in more colourful clothes.

32. The white horse corresponds to the 'spirited', or *thumoeides*,
    part as described in the *Republic*; by comparison, it is signally
    under-described in the *Phaedrus*, which may or may not be a
    reason for suspecting an intertextual reference.

33. For the full significance of the difference between what I here
    identify as the *Symposium* and *Phaedrus* models of the soul, see
    Rowe in Reshotko (ed.) 2003, and Penner and Rowe forth-
    coming. (The *Lysis* contains the fullest account anywhere in the
    dialogues of the '*Symposium* model'.) To the modern mind, as
    indeed to Aristotle's, the *Phaedrus* model is the obvious choice
    between the two: see e.g. Price 1995 and 1997, and Lear 1993.
    Penner and Rowe forthcoming, however, will take a different
    line.

Further Reading

Annas, Julia, and Christopher Rowe (eds), *New Perspectives on Plato, Modern and Ancient* (Cambridge, MA: Harvard University Press, 2002)

Blondell, Ruby, *The Play of Character in Plato's Dialogues* (Cambridge: Cambridge University Press, 2002). Thought-provoking on the general issue of the relationship between the philosophical, literary and dramatic elements in the dialogues, though has disappointingly little to say about the *Phaedrus* itself.

Burger, Ronna, *Plato's Phaedrus: A Defense of a Philosophic Art of Writing* (Birmingham: University of Alabama Press, 1980

Burnet, John, *Platonis opera*, 5 vols. (Oxford Classical Texts), (Oxford: Clarendon Press, 1903), II

Burnyeat, Myles F. 'Socratic Midwifery, Platonic Inspiration', *Bulletin of the Institute of Classical Studies* 24 (1977), pp. 7–17; reprinted in Hugh H. Benson (ed.), *Essays on the Philosophy of Socrates* (Oxford: Oxford University Press, 1992), pp. 53–65

Cole, Thomas, *The Origins of Rhetoric in Ancient Greece* (Baltimore: Johns Hopkins University Press, 1991)

Cooper, John M., *Plato: Complete Works* (Indianapolis: Hackett, 1997)

de Vries, G. J., *A Commentary on the Phaedrus of Plato* (Amsterdam: Hakkert, 1969)

Derrida, Jacques, 'Plato's Pharmacy' = *Dissemination*, trans. Barbara Johnson (London: Athlone Press, 1981), pp. 61–171. An essay that in sum – despite its influence among some readers of the *Phaedrus* – tells us rather more about Derrida than about the *Phaedrus*, or about Plato; see Seán Burke, *The Death and Return of the Author*, second edn (Edinburgh: Edinburgh University Press, 1998), chap. 3

Dover, K. J., *Greek Homosexuality*, second edn (Cambridge, MA: Harvard University Press, 1986)

Ferrari, G. R. F., *Listening to the Cicadas: A Study of Plato's Phaedrus* (Cambridge Classical Studies), (Cambridge: Cambridge University Press, 1987)

———, 'Platonic Love', in Richard Kraut (ed.), *The Cambridge Companion to Plato* (Cambridge: Cambridge University Press, 1992), pp. 248–76

Fine, Gail, *Plato I* and *II* (Oxford: Oxford University Press, 1999). A useful general collection of articles on Plato, including one by Richard Bett, 'Immortality and the Nature of the Soul in the *Phaedrus*', which helps analyse the *Phaedrus*'s argument for the soul's immortality.

Gill, Christopher, 'Platonic Love and Individuality', in A. Loizou and H. Lesser (eds), *Polis and Politics: Essays in Greek Moral and Political Philosophy* (Aldershot: Avebury Series in Philosophy, 1990), pp. 69–88

——— (trans.), *Plato: Symposium* (Harmondsworth: Penguin Books, 1999). The companion to the present volume.

Griswold, Charles L., Jr, *Self-Knowledge in Plato's Phaedrus* (New Haven: Yale University Press, 1986). New paperback edition published by Pennsylvania State University Press, University Park, PA, in 1996

Hackforth, R., *Plato's Phaedrus* (Cambridge: Cambridge University Press, 1932). Translation and commentary.

Halliwell, Stephen 'Forms of Address: Socratic Vocatives in Plato', in F. de Martino and A. H. Sommerstein (eds), *Lo spettacolo delle voci* (Bari: Laterza, 1995), Pt 2, pp. 87–121

Halperin, David M., 'Plato and Erotic Reciprocity', *Classical Antiquity* 5 (1986), pp. 60–80

———, 'Plato and the Metaphysics of Desire', *Proceedings of the Boston Area Colloquium for Ancient Philosophy* 5 (1989), pp. 27–52

———, 'Platonic *Erôs* and What Men Call Love', *Ancient Philosophy* 5 (1985), pp. 161–204

Hamilton, Walter (trans.), *Plato, Phaedrus & Letters VII and VIII* (Harmondsworth: Penguin Books, 1973). The precursor of the present volume. The latter excludes the two letters not just because of doubts about their authenticity (in fact I regard them both as certainly spurious), but because to include them tends to suggest that the, or a, primary focus of the *Phaedrus* too is somehow Plato himself – when he has done his level best to make himself invisible. 'The seventh and eighth letters ... provide fascinating glimpses into the contemporary power struggle in Sicily and evidence his failure to put into practice his theory of the philosopher-king' (Hamilton, on the back cover of the 1973 Penguin): but even if Plato had a 'theory of the philosopher-king', that he ever seriously contemplated trying to 'put [it] into practice' in Syracuse, and in the person of Dionysius II, seems in the highest degree implausible. However, the problems with the seventh letter do not start, or end, here.

Heath, Malcolm, 'The Unity of Plato's *Phaedrus*', *Oxford Studies in Ancient Philosophy* 7 (1987), pp. 150–73, 189–91. See also Rowe 1987 below.

Irwin, Terence, *Plato's Ethics* (Oxford: Oxford University Press, 1995)

Janaway, Christopher, *Images of Excellence: Plato's Critique of the Arts* (Oxford: Clarendon Press, 1995)

Kahn, Charles H., 'Plato's Theory of Desire', *Review of Metaphysics* 41 (1987), pp. 77–103

Kennedy, George, *The Art of Persuasion in Greece* (Princeton: Princeton University Press, 1963)

Kosman, L. A., 'Platonic Love', in W. Werkmeister (ed.), *Facets of Plato's Philosophy* (*Phronesis* Supplementary Volume 2) (Assen: Van Gorcum, 1976), pp. 53–69

Lear, Jonathan, 'Plato's Politics of Narcissism', in Terence Irwin and Martha C. Nussbaum (eds), *Virtue, Love and Form: Essays in Memory of Gregory Vlastos*, *Apeiron* 26/3–4 (1993), pp. 137–59

Mackenzie, Mary Margaret, 'Paradox in Plato's *Phaedrus*', *Proceedings of the Cambridge Philological Society* N. S. 28 (1982), pp. 64–76

Morgan, Kathryn, 'Socrates and Gorgias at Delphi and Olympia: *Phaedrus* 235d6–236b4', *Classical Quarterly*, N. S. 44/2 (1994), pp. 375–86

Moravcsik, Julius, and Philip Temko, *Plato on Beauty, Wisdom and the Arts* (Totowa, NJ: Rowman and Littlefield, 1982)

Nails, Debra, *The People of Plato* (Indianapolis: Hackett 2003). A complete account of what we can reconstruct about the people who figure in Plato's dialogues; indispensable.

Nehamas, Alexander, and Paul Woodruff (trans.), *Plato, Phaedrus* (Indianapolis: Hackett, 1995)

Nightingale, Andrea W., *Genres in Dialogue: Plato and the Construct of Philosophy* (Cambridge: Cambridge University Press, 1995)

Nussbaum, Martha C., *The Fragility of Goodness: Luck and Ethics in Greek Tragedy and Philosophy* (Cambridge: Cambridge University Press, 1986)

——, and Juha Sihvola (eds), *The Sleep of Reason: Erotic Experience and Sexual Ethics in Ancient Greece and Rome* (Chicago: University of Chicago Press, 2002)

Osborne, Catherine, *Eros Unveiled: Plato and the God of Love* (Oxford: Clarendon Press, 1994)

Pender, E. E., *Images of Persons Unseen: Plato's Metaphors for the Gods and the Soul* (Sankt Augustin: Academia Verlag (International Studies 11), 2000)

Penner, Terry, *The Ascent from Nominalism: Some Existence Arguments in Plato's Middle Dialogues* (Dordrecht: Reidel (Philosophical Studies Series 37), 1987)

——, 'Socrates and the Early Dialogues', in Richard Kraut (ed.), *The Cambridge Companion to Plato* (Cambridge: Cambridge University Press, 1992), pp. 121–69. An excellent short account of the Socratic theory of desire and action from which the *Phaedrus* seems radically to distance itself.

——, and Christopher Rowe, *Plato's Lysis* (Cambridge: Cambridge University Press, forthcoming). An interpretation of a puzzling dialogue – one of the 'early' ones referred to in the title of the preceding item – that deals with some of the main topics of both the *Phaedrus* and the *Symposium*.

Price, A. W., *Love and Friendship in Plato and Aristotle*

(Oxford: Clarendon Press, 1997). With important Afterword added to original 1989 edition.

———, *Mental Conflict* (London: Routledge (Issues in Ancient Philosophy), 1995)

Rowe, Christopher J., 'The Argument and Structure of Plato's *Phaedrus*', *Proceedings of the Cambridge Philological Society* 32 (1986), pp. 106–25

———, 'Philosophy, Love, and Madness', in Christopher Gill (ed.), *The Person and the Human Mind* (Oxford: Clarendon Press, 1990), pp. 227–46

———, *Plato*, second edn (London: Bristol Classical Paperbacks, 2003). An introduction to Plato that attempts to acknowledge the fact that he wrote *dialogues*.

———, 'Plato', in David Sedley, *Companion to Greek and Roman Philosophy* (Cambridge: Cambridge University Press, 2003), pp. 98–124

———, *Plato: Phaedrus* (Warminster: Aris & Phillips, 1986). Translation with facing Greek text and commentary.

———, 'Plato, Socrates and Developmentalism', in Naomi Reshotko (ed.), *Desire, Identity and Existence: Essays in Honour of T. M. Penner* (Kelowna, BC: Academic Printing and Publishing, 2003)

———, *Plato: Symposium* (Warminster: Aris & Phillips, 1996). Translation with facing Greek text and commentary.

———, 'The Unity of the *Phaedrus*: A Reply to Heath', *Oxford Studies in Ancient Philosophy* 7 (1987), pp. 175–88

Santas, Gerasimos X., *Goodness and Justice* (Oxford: Blackwell, 2001)

———, *Plato and Freud* (Oxford: Blackwell, 1988)

Szlezák, Thomas, *Reading Plato* (London: Routledge, 1999)

Vlastos, Gregory, *Socrates: Ironist and Moral Philosopher* (Ithaca, NY: Cornell University Press, 1991)

White, David A., *Rhetoric and Reality in Plato's Phaedrus* (Albany: State University of New York Press, 1993)

A Note on the Text and Translation

The Greek text translated in this volume is the same – barring some further changes to punctuation – as that translated in Rowe, *Plato: Phaedrus* (1986) – i.e. Burnet's Oxford text with a number of modifications.

The translation itself is also fundamentally the same as in the 1986 volume, but a close comparison will show that there have been numerous small-scale changes. The original version was written to go with a facing Greek text and a commentary. It was designed partly to help readers of the original find their way through what is frequently *difficult* Greek, partly to enable those without Greek to see something of the structure of the original. Further, with a commentary in support, the translation could sometimes share with it the job of communicating the sense of Plato's text to the reader. A translation that stands by itself – even with endnotes – needs to be a creature of a rather different, and more independent, sort. The new translation is also more like English than much of the 1986 version. However, I have still tried to keep something of the shape of the Greek, not least because in the course of the dialogue Plato adopts several different styles, which need to be presented to the reader if he or she is to have any chance of grasping properly what exactly Socrates – the main character – is up to at any given point, and in particular what *tone* he is using. Adapting the Greek, for example, to standard English sentence lengths, tends to obscure such variations. I make no apology, then, if the translation sometimes does not read quite like ordinary English prose. And it would be pointless to *apologize* if the English fails by a long way to reproduce the brilliance of Plato's language;

anyone who wants properly to appreciate that had better learn to read Greek.

I add, finally, that the translation, along with the Introduction and the notes, builds at every stage on my commentary in the 1986 volume, to which I refer for detailed justification for choices made in translation or, more generally, in interpretation. Inevitably, there are some issues, both particular and more general, on which I have changed my mind over the last twenty or so years; in such cases I regard my 1986 thoughts as superseded, and I am grateful to have had the opportunity to move on to a sounder and clearer view. But this for the most part applies to relatively minor points of translation – where I have had the advantage of being able to consult and cross-check with another modern English translation, that of Nehamas and Woodruff (1995), now also installed in the Hackett *Plato: Complete Works* (see Further Reading). On some occasions, I have moved in their direction; where we disagree, that is a matter of decision and not of oversight. (One such disagreement has already been noted in the Introduction.)

PHAEDRUS

SOCRATES My dear Phaedrus, where is it you're going, and where have you come from?

PHAEDRUS From Lysias, son of Cephalus,[1] Socrates; and I'm going for a walk outside the wall,[2] because I spent a long time sitting there – since sun-up. I'm doing what your friend and mine, Acumenus,[3] advises, and taking my walks along the country roads; he says that walking here is more refreshing than in the colonnades.

SOCRATES He's right to say so, my friend. So it seems Lysias was in the city.

PHAEDRUS Yes, at Epicrates' house, the one Morychus used to live in,[4] near the temple of Olympian Zeus.[5]

SOCRATES So then how did you spend your time? Obviously Lysias was feasting you all with his speeches?[6]

PHAEDRUS You'll find out about that if you have the leisure to walk and listen.

SOCRATES What? Don't you think I shall be likely to regard it – to quote Pindar[7] – as 'a thing above even want of leisure', to hear how you and Lysias spent your time?

PHAEDRUS Well then – lead on.

SOCRATES Please tell me.

PHAEDRUS Certainly, Socrates, and it will be pretty appropriate for you to hear, because the speech on which we were spending our time was, I tell you, in a certain sort of way about *love*.[8] Lysias has represented someone beautiful being propositioned but not by a lover – indeed, that's just the subtlety of his invention: he says that favours should be granted[9] to a man who is not in love rather than to one who is.

SOCRATES How admirable of Lysias! I only wish he would write that it should be to a poor man rather than a rich one, and an older rather than a younger man, and all the other things which belong to me and to most of us; *then* his speeches would be urbane, and for the general good.[10] I for one am so eager to hear it, in any case, that if your walk takes you to Megara, and you touch the wall with your foot and come back again, as Herodicus recommends,[11] I certainly won't be left behind.

PHAEDRUS Socrates, my good fellow, what do you mean? Do you think that I, an amateur, will be able to repeat from memory in a way worthy of Lysias what he, the cleverest of present writers, has put together at leisure over a long period of time? Far from it; though I'd like to be able to, more than I'd want to come into a stack of money.

SOCRATES Phaedrus – if I don't know Phaedrus, I've forgotten even who I am. But I do, and I haven't; I know perfectly well that when he heard Lysias' speech he did not hear it just once, but repeatedly asked him to go through it for him, and Lysias responded readily. But for Phaedrus not even that was enough, and in the end he borrowed the book and examined the things in it which he was most eager to look at, and doing this he sat from sun-up until he was tired and went for a walk, as *I* think – I'll swear by the Dog[12] it's true – knowing the speech quite off by heart, unless it was a rather long one. He was going outside the wall to practise it, when he met the very person who is sick with passion for hearing people speak[13] – and 'seeing, seeing him',[14] he was glad, because he would have a companion in his manic frenzy, and he told him to lead on. Then when the one in love with speeches asked him to speak, he put on a pose, as if not eager to speak; but in the end, even if no one wanted to listen, he meant to use force, and *would* speak. So you, Phaedrus, you just ask him to do here and now what he will soon do anyway.

PHAEDRUS For me, really much the best thing is to speak as I can, since it seems to me you won't let me go until I speak, somehow or other.

SOCRATES You have just the right idea about me.

PHAEDRUS So that's what I'll do. Nothing could be truer,   d1
Socrates – I didn't learn it word for word; but I shall run
through the purport of just about everything in which he said
the situation of the lover was different from that of the non-
lover, giving a summary of each point in turn, beginning with   d5
the first.

SOCRATES Yes, my dear fellow, after you've first shown me
just what it is you have in your left hand under your cloak; for
I suspect you have the speech itself. If you have, you must know
this about me, that fond as I am of you, if Lysias is here as well,   e1
I am not really inclined to offer myself to you to practise on.
Come on, show me!

PHAEDRUS Stop! I'd hoped to flex my muscles on you, and
now you've foiled me![15] Well, where would you like us to sit   e5
down and read?

SOCRATES Let's turn off here and go along the Ilissus;[16] then   229a
we'll sit down quietly wherever we think best.

PHAEDRUS It seems it's just as well I happen to be barefoot;
you always are. So we can very easily go along the stream with   a5
our feet in the water; and it won't be unpleasant, particularly
at this time of year and of the day.

SOCRATES Lead on, then, and keep a lookout for a place for
us to sit down.

PHAEDRUS Well, you see that very tall plane-tree?

SOCRATES Of course.

PHAEDRUS There's shade and a moderate breeze there, and   b1
grass to sit on, or lie on, if we like.

SOCRATES Please lead on.

PHAEDRUS Tell me, Socrates, wasn't it from somewhere here
that Boreas is said to have seized Oreithuia[17] from the Ilissus?   b5

SOCRATES Yes, so it's said.

PHAEDRUS Well, was it from here? The rivulets look attractively pure and clear – just right for young girls to play beside.

SOCRATES No, it was from a place two or three stades lower   c1
down, where one crosses over to the district of Agra;[18] and
there, somewhere, there's an altar of Boreas.

PHAEDRUS I've not really noticed it. But do tell me, Socrates,   c5
for goodness' sake,[19] do you believe this fairy-tale to be true?

SOCRATES If I disbelieved it, as wise people[20] do, I'd not be extraordinary; then I'd use their wisdom and say that a blast of Boreas pushed her down from the nearby rocks while she was playing with Pharmaceia, and when she met her death in this

d1 way she was said to have been snatched up by Boreas – or else it was from the Areopagus; for this too is something people say, that it was from there and not from here that she was seized. But, Phaedrus, while I think such explanations attractive in other respects, they belong in my view to an over-clever and

d5 laborious person who is not altogether fortunate; just because after that he must set the shape of the Centaurs to rights, and again that of the Chimaera, and a mob of such things – Gorgons

e1 and Pegasuses – and strange hordes of other intractable and portentous kinds of creatures flock in on him; if someone is sceptical about these, and tries with his boorish kind of wisdom to reduce each to what is likely, he'll need a good deal of leisure.

e5 As for me, there's no way I have leisure for it all, and the reason for it, my friend, is this. I am not yet capable of 'knowing myself', in accordance with the Delphic inscription;[21] so it seems

230a absurd to me that while I am still ignorant of this subject I should inquire into things which do not belong to me. So then saying goodbye to these things, and believing what is commonly thought about them, as I was saying just now, I inquire not into these but into myself, to see whether I am actually a beast

a5 more complex and more typhonic than Typhon,[22] or both a tamer and a simpler creature, sharing by nature some divine and un-typhonic portion. But, my friend, to interrupt our conversation,[23] wasn't this the tree you were taking us to?

b1 PHAEDRUS It's the very one.

SOCRATES By Hera, a beautiful stopping-place![24] The plane-tree here is altogether spreading and tall, and the tallness and shadiness of the *agnus castus*[25] are quite lovely; it's at the peak

b5 of its flowering and gives the place the sweetest perfume it could. The stream, too, flows very attractively under the plane, with the coolest water, to judge by my foot. To judge by the figurines and statuettes, the spot seems to be sacred to some

c1 nymphs and to Achelous.[26] Then again, if you like, how welcome it is, the freshness of the place, and very pleasant; it echoes

with a summery shrillness to the cicadas' song. Most charming
of all is the matter of the grass, growing on a gentle slope and
thick enough to be just right to rest one's head upon. So you've   c5
been the best of guides for a stranger, my dear Phaedrus.

PHAEDRUS You, my friend, really appear the most extraordinary[27] sort of person. You behave like someone being led
around a strange place, as you say, and not like a local. It comes   d1
of your not leaving the city to cross the border or even, it seems
to me, to go outside the wall at all.

SOCRATES Forgive me, my good man. You see, I'm a lover of
learning, and country places and trees won't teach me anything,   d5
which the people of the city[28] will. But you seem to have found
the prescription[29] to get me to go out. Just like people who
lead hungry animals on by waving a branch or some kind of
vegetable in front of them, so you seem to me to be going to
lead me round all of Attica and wherever else you please by   e1
doing as you are now and proffering me speeches in books.[30]
In any case, now that I've got here, I think I'm going to lie
down for the present, and you choose whatever pose you think
easiest for reading, and read.

PHAEDRUS Listen, then.[31]   e5

'How it is with me, you know, and how I think it is to our
advantage that these things[32] should happen, you have heard
me say; and I claim that I should not fail to achieve the things   231a
I ask for because I happen not to be in love with you. Those in
love repent of whatever services they do at the point they cease
from their desire; for the others, there is no time appropriate
for repentance. For it is not under compulsion but at their own   a5
choosing, and in accordance with the way they would best
look after their own affairs, that they render *their* services, in
proportion to their own capacity.[33] Again, those who are in
love consider the damage they did to their own interests because
of their love and the services they have performed and, adding
in the labour they have put in, they think they have long since   b1
given return enough to the objects of their love; whereas those
not in love cannot allege neglect of their own interests because
of it, nor reckon up their past labours, nor put the blame on
quarrels with their relatives. So with all these bad things   b5

removed, there is nothing left but to perform readily whatever actions they think will please the other party.[34] Again, if it is

c1 worth putting a high value on those in love because they say they show the greatest degree of affection to those they are in love with, and are ready to incur the enmity of everyone else for their words[35] and actions if it only pleases their beloved, it

c5 is easy to see, if they are telling the truth, that they'll put a higher value on those they fall in love with later than they put on *them*, and clear too that they will maltreat them at the bidding of their new loves. Yet how is it reasonable to give

d1 away such a thing[36] to someone in so unfortunate a condition – one that no person with experience of it would even try to prevent? For the ones who suffer it agree themselves that they are sick rather than in their right mind, and that they *know* they are out of their mind but cannot control themselves; so

d5 how, when they come to their senses, could they approve of the decisions they make when in this condition? Moreover, if you were to choose the best one out of those in love with you, your choice would be only from a few, while if you chose the most suitable to yourself out of everybody else, you would be choos-

e1 ing from many; so that you would have a much greater expectation of chancing on the man worthy of your affection[37] among the many.

'Now if you are afraid of established convention, that if

232a people find out you will be subject to censure, the likelihood is that those in love, thinking they would be envied by everyone else, too, just as they envy themselves, will be on tiptoe with talking about it and boastfully display to all and sundry that they have not laboured in vain; whereas those not in love,

a5 because they are in control of themselves, will choose what is best rather than to have people think highly of them. And again, many are bound to find out about those in love because they see them following their loved ones around and making a prac-

b1 tice of it, so that when they are seen in conversation with each other, people think that they are together in the context of passion spent or soon to be spent; whereas no one even tries to blame those not in love for their being together, because they

b5 know people have to talk if they are friends or to get any other

sort of pleasure. Moreover, if you are frightened by the thought
that it is difficult for affection to last, and that while under
other circumstances the occurrence of a quarrel is a misfortune
shared by both parties, if you have given away what you value   c1
most it is on *you* that great injury would be inflicted, in that
case you will have reason to fear those in love more, for there
are many things that cause them pain, and everything, they
think, is done in order to inflict injury on them. It is for this   c5
very reason that they divert their loved ones from associating
with others, fearing that those who possess wealth will outdo
them with their money, and that the educated will come off
better in terms of intellect; and they are on their guard against
the power of anyone who possesses any other sort of advantage.   d1
So by having persuaded you to become an object of hatred to
these people, they isolate you from any friends and, if you
consider your own interest and show more sense than they do,
you will come into conflict with them; whereas those who
happened not to be in love, but achieved what they asked   d5
through merit, would not begrudge those who associate with
the objects of their attentions but would hate those who did
not wish to do so, thinking that they were being looked down
on by the latter but benefited by the presence of the former, so
that there is much greater expectation that the other party will   e1
gain friends than enemies from the affair.

'Moreover, many of those in love desire a person's body
before they know his ways and before they have experience of   e5
the other aspects belonging to him, so that it is unclear to them
if they will still want to be friends with him when they cease to
desire him; whereas for those not in love, since they were friends   233a
with each other even before they did what they did, whatever
benefits they receive[38] are not likely to make their friendship
less but rather to be left as reminders of what is still to come.
Moreover, you should expect to become a better person if you   a5
listen to my arguments than if you listen to a lover's. For lovers
praise words and actions even if it means disregarding what is
best, in part because they are afraid of being hated, in part
because their own judgement is weakened as a result of their   b1
desire. For such are the ways that love displays itself: if lovers

are unsuccessful, it makes them regard as distressing the sorts
of things that cause pain to no one else; if they are successful,
love compels them to praise even things which ought not to
b5 cause pleasure at all; so that it is much more fitting for their
loved ones to pity them than to want to emulate them. But if
you listen to me, in the first place I shall give you my company
c1 with an eye not to present pleasure but also to the benefit that
is to come, not being overcome by love but mastering myself,
and not starting violent hostility because of small things but
feeling slight anger slowly because of big ones, forgiving the
c5 unintentional and trying to prevent the intentional; for these
are signs of a friendship that will last for a long time. But if,
after all, you have the thought that strong friendship cannot
d1 occur unless a man is actually in love, you should bear in mind
that in that case we would neither value our sons nor our
fathers and mothers, nor would we have trustworthy friends,
who are the product not of desire of this sort but of practices
of a different kind.

d5   'And again, if it were the rule that one should grant favours
most to those who are most in need of them, then the rest of
mankind too ought to benefit not the best people but the most
helpless; for since they will have been released from the greatest
sufferings, they will be the most grateful to their benefactors.
e1 Moreover, when it comes to private expenditure too, it will be
right to invite, not one's friends, but those who beg for their
share and those who need filling up; for they will treat their
benefactors fondly, attend on them, call at their doors, feel the
e5 most delight and not the least gratitude, and pray for many
good things for them. Yet perhaps the fitting thing is rather to
grant favours not to those who stand in great need of them but
to those who are most able to pay a favour back; not to those
234a who are merely in love with you but to those who deserve the
thing you have to give; not to the sort who will take advantage
of your youthful beauty but to the ones who will share their
own advantages with you when you become older; not to those
who after they have achieved their aim will boast of it to
a5 everyone else but to the ones who will say nothing to anyone,
out of a sense of shame; not to those who are devoted to you

for a short time but to those whose friendship for you will remain unaltered throughout their whole life; not to the ones who will look for an excuse for hostilities with you when they cease to desire you but those who will display their own excellence at that very moment when you cease to be in the   b1 prime of youth. So I say to you: Remember what has been said, and bear this in mind: that those in love are admonished by their friends on the basis that what they do is bad, whereas those not in love have never been blamed by anyone close to them for making bad decisions because of that about their own   b5 interests.

'You will perhaps ask me, then, whether I advise you to grant favours to all those who are not in love with you. I for my part think that not even the man who was in love with you would tell you to take this attitude to all those who were. For neither   c1 would it merit equal gratitude from the receiver nor would it be possible for you to keep things secret from everyone else in the same way, if you wished to do so; but from the thing[39] no harm should come, only benefit to both parties.

'So I think what I have said is sufficient; but if there is   c5 something you miss[40] in my arguments and think I have left out, ask me about it.'

How does the speech seem to you, Socrates? Doesn't it seem to you to be extraordinarily well done, especially in its language?

SOCRATES Superhumanly, in fact, my friend; enough to make   d1 me beside myself. And it was because of you, Phaedrus, that I felt as I did, as I looked at you, because you seemed to me to be positively beaming with delight at the speech as you read it; for I followed your lead, thinking that you are more of an   d5 expert about such things than me, and I joined in the ecstasy with your inspired[41] self.

PHAEDRUS Just stop. Do you mean to joke about it like this?

SOCRATES Do I really seem to you to be joking and not serious?

PHAEDRUS Don't do that, Socrates. Tell me really – in the name   e1 of Zeus, the god of friendship – do you think any other Greek who gave his own speech on the same subject would have weightier and more numerous things to say?

e5 SOCRATES What? Should you and I also praise the speech on the grounds that its creator[42] has said what he should, and not just because he has said things clearly and in a well-rounded fashion, and each and every word of his is precisely turned? If we should, then I must go along with your judgement, for your

235a sake, though in fact I missed it[43] through my feebleness; for I was only paying attention to the rhetorical aspect of the speech. In this other respect I didn't think even Lysias himself thought the speech adequate; and in fact he seemed to me, Phaedrus, unless you say otherwise, to have said the same things two or

a5 three times over, as if he wasn't altogether well off when it came to saying many things about the same subject, or else perhaps because he didn't care at all about this sort of thing; indeed he seemed to me to be behaving with a youthful swagger, showing off his ability to say the same things now in this way and now in that, and to say them excellently either way.

b1 PHAEDRUS You're talking nonsense, Socrates; the very thing you mention is in fact the main feature of the speech. It has left out nothing that was waiting in the subject to be expressed in a way worthy of it; so that no one could ever say other things

b5 which were more numerous and of greater worth than what *he* said.

SOCRATES That's where I shall no longer be able to go along with you; men and women of old, wise people who have spoken and written about the subject, will refute me if I agree as a favour to you.

c1 PHAEDRUS Who are these people? And where have you heard better things than there are in Lysias' speech?

SOCRATES At the moment I can't say, just like that, but clearly I *have* heard something,[44] either – maybe – from the beautiful Sappho, or from Anacreon the wise, or indeed from some

c5 prose-writers.[45] On what evidence do I say this? My breast is full, if I may say so, my fine fellow, and I see that I would have other things to say beyond what Lysias says, and no worse either. I am well aware that I have thought up none of them from within *my* resources, because I am conscious of my own ignorance; the only alternative, then, I think, is that I have been

d1 filled up through my ears, like a vessel, from someone else's streams. But dullness again has made me forget this very thing, how I heard it and from whom.

PHAEDRUS Absolutely excellent![46] I love what I hear. Don't you tell me from whom and how you heard it, not even if I tell you to, but do exactly as you say: you've promised to say better things and no fewer than those in the book – different things, and keeping away from what Lysias says; and I in my turn promise you that like the nine archons[47] I'll dedicate a golden statue of equal weight at Delphi, not just of me but of you as well.

SOCRATES You are a very dear man, and truly made of gold, Phaedrus, if you think I mean that Lysias has completely missed the mark, and that I'm actually able to say different things, beyond everything he says; that couldn't, I think, happen even to the worst writer. To begin with, on the topic of the speech, who do you think – if he is saying that one should grant favours to the one who is not in love rather than to the one who is – would be able not to laud the good sense of the one and censure the lack of sense of the other, these being indispensable points, and then have something further to say? In my view such points must be allowed, and one should be forgiven for making them; with such things, what should be praised is not so much the invention as the arrangement, whereas with things that are not indispensable, and are difficult to invent, we should praise the invention as well as the arrangement.

PHAEDRUS I agree with what you say; it seems a reasonable statement. So for my part, I'll behave like this: I'll allow you to make it an assumption that the man in love is more sick than the man not in love; but when you've made a speech different from Lysias' in all other respects, and one that contains more points and of greater worth, then you'll stand in hammered metal beside the dedication of the Cypselids at Olympia.[48]

SOCRATES Have you been taking me seriously, Phaedrus, because I made my teasing attack on your darling? Do you think I would really try to say something different, of greater variety, to set beside his wisdom?

PHAEDRUS Now here, my friend, you've really let me catch you. You'll have to say your piece, however you can, to avoid our being forced to behave in the vulgar way we see on the comic stage, exchanging jibes; watch out, and don't deliberately

c5 make me give you a 'Socrates, if I don't know Socrates, I've even forgotten who *I* am,' or a 'he was desperate to speak, but put on a pose.' Just make up your mind that we won't leave this spot until you say what you were claiming you had 'in your

d1 breast'. We're alone in a deserted place, and I'm stronger and younger than you; from all of which 'grasp the meaning of my words',[49] and make sure you're not forced to speak when you can do it voluntarily.

SOCRATES But, Phaedrus, my fine friend – I shall be a laughing-

d5 stock if I improvise as a layman in competition with an expert craftsman[50] on the same subjects.

PHAEDRUS I warn you, stop being coy with me. I've got something to say which will pretty well force you to speak.

SOCRATES Then don't say it.

d10 PHAEDRUS No, I shall say it, and what I say will be an oath. I

e1 swear to you – but by whom, by which god? What about this plane-tree here? I swear that if you don't make your speech *in the presence of this tree*, I shall neither display nor report to you any speech of anyone's ever again.

SOCRATES You wretch, you! How well you've found the way

e5 to force a lover of speeches to do whatever you tell him to do.

PHAEDRUS So why go on twisting and turning?

SOCRATES Not any longer, now you've sworn what you've sworn. How would I be able to keep myself away from feasts of that sort?

237a PHAEDRUS Speak then.

SOCRATES Do you know what I shall do, then?

PHAEDRUS About what?

SOCRATES I shall speak with my head covered, so that I can

a5 rush through my speech as quickly as I can and not lose my way through shame, from looking at you.

PHAEDRUS Just speak; for the rest, do as you like.

SOCRATES Come then, you Muses, whether you are 'clear-voiced' because of the beauty of your song, or whether you acquired this epithet through the musical race of the Ligurians,[51]

a10 'take part with me'[52] in the story this excellent fellow here

forces me to tell, so that his friend,[53] who seemed to him to be   b1
wise even before, may seem even more so now.

'Once upon a time, then, there was a boy, or rather a young
lad, and very beautiful he was; and he had a very large number
of lovers. And one of them was cunning, because although he
was as much in love as any of them, he had convinced the boy
that he was not in love with him. And once in pressing his   b5
claims he tried to convince him of just this, that one ought to
grant favours to one not in love rather than to the one in love;
and he spoke like this:

'"In everything, my boy, there is one starting-point for those
who are going to deliberate successfully: they must know what   c1
they are deliberating about, or they will inevitably miss their
target altogether. Most people are unaware that they do not
know what each thing really is.[54] So then, assuming that they
know what it is, they fail to reach agreement about it at the
beginning of their enquiry, and, having gone forward on this
basis, they pay the penalty one would expect: they agree neither   c5
with themselves nor with each other. So let us, you and I, avoid
having happen to us what we find fault with in others: since
the discussion before you and me is whether one should rather
enter into friendship with lover or with non-lover, let us establish an agreed definition of love, about what sort of thing it is   d1
and what power it possesses, and look to this as our point of
reference while we make our enquiry as to whether it brings
help or harm.

'"Well then, that love is some sort of desire[55] is clear to
everyone; and again we know that men desire the beautiful[56]   d5
even if they are not in love. By what then shall we distinguish
the man in love and the man who is not? Our next step is to
observe that in each of us there are two kinds of thing which
rule and lead us, which we follow wherever they may lead,
the one an inborn desire for pleasures, the other an acquired
judgement that aims at the best. These two things in us are
sometimes in accord, but there are times when they are at   e1
variance; and sometimes the one, at other times the second, has
control. Now when judgement leads us by reason towards the
best and is in control, its control over us has the name of

238a   restraint;[57] when desire drags us irrationally towards pleasures
       and has established rule within us, its rule is called by the name
       of excess.[58] Excess is something which has many names, for it
       has many limbs and many forms; and whichever of these forms
  a5   happens to stand out in any case, it gives its possessor its own
       name, which is neither an admirable one nor one worth the
       acquisition. When it is in connection with food that a desire
       has achieved control over both reasoning for the best and the
  b1   other desires, it is called gluttony, and will give its possessor
       this same name; again, when it has become a tyrant in connec-
       tion with drinking, leading the man who has acquired it in this
       direction, it is plain what appellation he will receive; and as for
  b5   the other related names of related desires, we can see already
       that a person will be called by the appropriate one, that of
       whichever desire happens at any time to be in power. As for
       the desire for the sake of which all the foregoing has been said,
       it is already pretty evident what one should say; but everything
       is in a way clearer when said than when unsaid: the irrational
       desire that has gained control over any judgement urging a man
  c1   towards what is correct, and that is carried towards pleasure
       in beauty – in turn being forcefully reinforced by the desires
       related to it in its pursuit of the beauty of bodies – and that
       wins victory by its drive, taking its name from its very force:
       this is called love." '[59]

  c5   Well then, my dear Phaedrus, do you think, as I do myself,
       that something more than human[60] has happened to me?
       PHAEDRUS I certainly agree, Socrates, that you've been seized
       by a fluency greater than normal.
       SOCRATES Then listen to me in silence. For the spot seems
  d1   really to be a divine one, so if by any chance I become possessed
       by Nymphs as my speech proceeds, don't be surprised; as it is,
       I'm already close to uttering in dithyrambs.[61]
       PHAEDRUS Very true.
  d5   SOCRATES For that you're to blame. But listen to what remains;
       perhaps the threat might be averted. That, though, will be a
       matter for god; we must return to the boy with our speech.

            ' "Well, my brave friend:[62] we have stated, then, and defined
       what it really is that is to be deliberated about; so, looking

towards that, let us say, for the rest, what help or harm will be   e1
likely to accrue to the person granting favours, from lover and
non-lover. Now it is necessarily[63] the case, I suppose, that the
man who is ruled by desire and enslaved to pleasure will make
the one he loves as pleasing to himself as possible; and to a sick
man anything which does not resist him is pleasant, while   e5
anything which is stronger than he is or equal to him is hateful.
 So a lover will not willingly put up with his beloved's being   239a
stronger than him or matching him but always tries to make
him weaker and less self-sufficient; and an ignorant man is
weaker than a wise one, a coward than a brave man, a poor
speaker than an expert in rhetoric, a slow-witted man than a
quick one. When all these faults and more besides make their   a5
appearance or are present by nature in the mind of a loved one,
a lover will necessarily delight in these and procure others,
or else he will be deprived of what is immediately pleasant.
Necessarily, then, he will be jealous, and by keeping him from   b1
many other forms of association, of a beneficial kind, which
would most make a man of him, he will be a cause of great
harm to him; and he will be the cause of the greatest harm by
keeping him from that association from which he would
become *wisest*.[64] This is what that divine thing, philosophy, is,
from which the lover must necessarily keep his beloved far   b5
away, out of a dread of being despised; and he must contrive
in everything else that the boy should be in complete ignorance
and looking for everything to his lover, which is the condition
in which he will offer most pleasure to the other but most harm
to himself. So, in respect of the mind, there is no profit at all in   c1
a man as guardian and partner if he is in love.
 ' "What we must look at after this is the condition of the
body and its treatment: what sort of physical condition will the
man who is under compulsion to pursue pleasure in preference
to good aim to produce in anyone under his charge, and what   c5
treatment will he apply? And he will be observed pursuing
someone soft and not tough, brought up not in the full light of
the sun but in a dappled shade, unversed in manly exertions
and harsh, sweated labour but fully versed in a soft and effemi-
nate way of life, decking himself out in borrowed colours and   d1

ornaments for lack of his own, and resorting to all the other
practices that go along with these, which are obvious and are
not worth listing further but will allow us to go on to another
matter after we have laid down one summary point: a body in
d5   such condition is one that in war and in other times of great
crisis gives heart to the enemy, and creates alarm in one's
friends, and in one's lovers themselves.

'"This, then, we should dismiss as obvious, and pass on to
e1   the point that comes next: what help or what harm to us in
respect of our possessions the society and guardianship of the
man in love will bring. This at least is clear enough to everyone,
and especially to the lover: that he would pray above all for the
e5   one he loves to be bereft of his dearest and best-intentioned and
most divine possessions; for he would be happy for him to be
240a deprived of father and mother, relations and friends, thinking
them likely to prevent and censure the most pleasant kind of
intercourse he has with him. Further, if his loved one possesses
property, in the form of gold or any other possession, he will
think him neither as easy to catch nor as manageable once
caught; as a result, there is every necessity that the lover should
a5   begrudge his beloved the possession of his property, and delight
in his loss of it. So too the lover would pray that his beloved
should be without wife, without children, without home for the
longest possible time, because he desires to reap the sweetness of
his own enjoyment for as long as possible.

'"There are indeed other bad things in life, but with most of
b1   them some divine agency mixes a pleasure of the moment: so
with the flatterer, a formidable beast and a source of great
harm, nature has nevertheless mixed in a certain pleasure that
is not entirely gross; and one might object to a courtesan as
something harmful, and many other similarly endowed crea-
b5   tures and their practices, which have the feature of being very
pleasant, at least to meet the needs of the day. But for the
beloved, the lover, over and above his harmfulness, is the least
c1   pleasant of all things to spend the day with. As the proverb has
it too, 'young delights young' – for I suppose matching years
draw people to matching pleasures and so makes them friends
on the grounds of likeness; yet all the same, even these are

bound to have enough of being together. What is more, in every
sphere what is *compulsory* is said to be oppressive to everyone;   c5
and this element is especially present in the relation of lover to
beloved, in addition to their dissimilarity. The older man does
not willingly let the younger one leave his company, whether
by day or by night, but is driven by a frenzied compulsion that   d1
draws him on, by giving *him* pleasures all the time, as he sees,
hears, touches, experiences his loved one through all the senses,
so that pleasure makes him press his services on him; but as for
the one who is loved, what kind of solace or what pleasures   d5
will the lover give *him*, to prevent *him*, when he is with him over
that same period of time, from experiencing extreme disgust –
when he sees a face that is old and past its prime, along with
everything else which follows on that, which it is no pleasure   e1
even to hear talked about, let alone be continually compelled
actually to deal with; when he is guarded suspiciously all the
time and in all his relationships; and when he hears himself
praised at the wrong times, and too much, and reproached in just
the same way, which is intolerable when his lover is sober but   e5
shaming as well as intolerable when he is drunk and speaking
with an unrestrained and barefaced licence?

'"And while he is in love, the lover is harmful and unpleasant,
but when he ceases to be in love there is no trusting him in
relation to the future, for which he promised many things with   e10
many oaths and entreaties, so barely prevailing on the other   241a
one in that previous time to put up with his company, painful
as it was, through hope of goods to come. Then, at the point
when he should be paying back what he owes, he substitutes a
different ruler and champion in himself, sense and sanity in
place of love and madness, and has become a different person
without his beloved's realizing it. And the beloved asks for   a5
something in return for what happened before,[65] giving reminders of what was done and said then, thinking that he is
talking to the same man; while the other through shame cannot
either bring himself to say that he has become a different person
or see his way to making good the oaths and promises of his
previous mindless regime, having now come to his senses and   b1
sobered up[66] – for fear that if he did the same things as his

previous self, he would become like that self again, the same
person. A fugitive, then, is what he becomes from all of this,
b5 and, compelled to default, the former lover changes direction
and launches himself into flight as the sherd flips on to its other
side;[67] and the other one is compelled to run after him, angrily
invoking the gods, ignorant of everything from the beginning:
that in fact he ought never to have granted favours to one in
c1 love and necessarily[68] mindless but much rather to one who
was not in love and who was in possession of his senses; and that
otherwise he was necessarily surrendering himself to someone
untrustworthy, peevish, jealous, disagreeable, harmful to property, harmful to his physical condition, but by far most harmful
c5 to the education of his soul, than which in truth there neither
is nor ever will be anything more valuable in the eyes either of
men or of gods. So these, my boy, are the things you must bear
in mind, and you must understand that the friendship of a lover
does not come with goodwill; it's like an appetite for food, for
d1 the purpose of filling up – as wolves love lambs, so is lovers'
affection for a boy." '[69]

There, Phaedrus, it's as I said it would be.[70] You'll hear nothing
further than that from me; please let my speech end here.

PHAEDRUS But I thought it was just in the middle, and would
d5 go on to say an equal amount about the non-lover, to the effect
that one should rather grant him favours, saying all the good
things he has on *his* side; why are you stopping now?

e1 SOCRATES Haven't you noticed, my fine fellow, that I'm already
uttering epic verses, no longer dithyrambs now, even though
I'm playing the critic?[71] What do you think I'll produce if I
begin praising the other man? Don't you know I'll patently be
e5 possessed by the Nymphs, to whom *you* deliberately exposed
me? So, in a word, I say that the other man has the good points
that are opposed to all the things for which we've abused the
first. And why indeed make a long speech of it? Enough has
been said about both. So whatever fate should befall my story
242a will befall it without me;[72] I'm off across the river here before
I'm forced by you into something bigger.

PHAEDRUS Don't go yet, Socrates, not until the heat of the day
has passed. Don't you see that it's just about midday, the time[73]

when we say everything stands still? Let's wait and discuss a5
what's been said, and then we'll go, when it's cooler.

SOCRATES You've a superhuman capacity[74] when it comes to
speeches, Phaedrus; you're simply amazing. Of the speeches
there have been during your lifetime, I think no one has brought b1
more into existence than you, either by making them yourself
or by forcing others to make them, in one way or another.
Simmias the Theban[75] is the one exception; the rest you beat by
a long way. Just so, now, I think you've again become the cause
of my making a speech. b5

PHAEDRUS No bad thing! But how do you mean? What speech
is this?

SOCRATES When I was about to cross the river, my good
man, I had that supernatural experience, the sign[76] that I am
accustomed to having – on each occasion, you understand, it c1
holds me back from whatever I am about to do – and I seemed
to hear a kind of voice from the very spot, forbidding me to
leave until I make expiation, because I have committed an
offence against what belongs to the gods.[77] Well, I am a seer;
not a very good one, but like people who are poor at reading c5
and writing, just good enough for my own purposes; so I
already clearly understand what my offence is. For the fact is,
my friend, that the soul too is something which has divinatory
powers; for something certainly troubled me some while ago as
I was making the speech, and I had a certain feeling of unease,
as Ibycus says (if I remember rightly), 'that for offences against d1
the gods, I win renown from all my fellow men'.[78] But now I
realize my offence.

PHAEDRUS Just what do you mean?

SOCRATES A dreadful speech it was, Phaedrus, dreadful, both
the one you brought with you and the one you compelled me d5
to make.

PHAEDRUS How so?

SOCRATES It was foolish and somewhat impious; what speech
could be more dreadful than that?

PHAEDRUS None – if you're right in what you say.

SOCRATES What? Don't you think Love to be the son of
Aphrodite, and a god?

dɪo PHAEDRUS So it is said.

SOCRATES Not, I think, by Lysias, at any rate, nor by your
eɪ speech, which came from my mouth, bewitched as it was by
your potion.[79] But if Love is, as indeed he is, a god, or something
divine, he would not be anything bad; whereas the two speeches
we had just now spoke of him as if he were like that. So
e5 this was their offence in relation to Love; and besides, their
foolishness was really quite refined – parading themselves as
243a if they were worth something while actually saying nothing
healthy or true, in case they might deceive some poor specimens
of humanity and win praise from them. So I, my friend, must
purify myself, and for those who offend in the telling of stories
there is an ancient method of purification, which Homer was
a5 not aware of, but Stesichorus[80] was. For when he was deprived
of his sight because of his libel against Helen, he did not fail to
recognize the cause, like Homer; because he was a true follower
of the Muses,[81] he knew it, and immediately composed the
verses

> This tale I told is false. There is no doubt:
> You made no journey in the well-decked ships
bɪ > Nor voyaged to the citadel of Troy.[82]

And after composing the whole of the so-called *Palinode*,[83] he
at once regained his sight. So I shall follow a wiser course than
Stesichorus and Homer in just this respect: I shall try to render
b5 my palinode to Love before anything happens to me because of
my libel against him, with my head bare, and not covered as it
was before, for shame.

PHAEDRUS There's nothing, Socrates, you could have said that
would have given me more pleasure.

cɪ SOCRATES Yes, my good Phaedrus, for you see how shamelessly
said the speeches were, this second one and the one from the
book. If we were being listened to by someone of a noble and
gentle character who was in love with someone else of the same
sort, or else had ever been in love with someone like that before,
c5 and he heard us saying that lovers start large-scale hostilities
because of small things, and adopt a jealous and harmful atti-

tude towards their beloved, surely you think he would suppose himself to be listening to people who had perhaps been brought up among sailors, and who had never seen a love of the sort that belongs to free men,[84] and would be far from agreeing with   d1
the things we find to blame in Love?

PHAEDRUS Zeus! Socrates, perhaps he would.

SOCRATES Then out of shame for what this man would think, and out of fear of Love himself, I for my part am anxious to wash away the bitter taste, as it were, of the things we have heard said, with a wholesome speech; and I advise Lysias too   d5
to put it in writing as quickly as possible that one should grant favours to a lover rather than to one not in love, in return for favours received.[85]

PHAEDRUS You can be sure that's how it will be: once you have spoken your praise of the lover, there'll be nothing for it but for me to compel Lysias to write a speech in his turn on the   e1
same subject.

SOCRATES I believe you'll do it; that's the sort of person you are.

PHAEDRUS Then you can give your speech with full confidence.

SOCRATES Where, then, is that boy I was talking to? I want him to hear this speech too; if he doesn't, he may go ahead and   e5
grant favours to the non-lover before we can stop him.

PHAEDRUS Here he is right next to you, whenever you wish.[86]

SOCRATES Well then, my beautiful boy, you should take note of this – that the previous speech belonged to Phaedrus son of   244a
Pythocles, of the deme Myrrhinous; while the one I am going to make belongs to Stesichorus son of Euphemus, of Himera.[87]
It must go like this: "The story is not true" if it says that when a lover is there for the having, one should rather grant favours to the one not in love, on the grounds that the first is mad,   a5
while the second is sane. That would be rightly said if it were a simple truth that madness is a bad thing; but as it is, the greatest of goods come to us through madness, provided that it is bestowed by divine gift. The prophetess at Delphi, no less, and the priestesses at Dodona do many fine things for Greece   b1
when mad, both on a private and on a public level, whereas when sane they achieve little or nothing; and if we speak of the

Sibyl and of others who by means of inspired prophecy foretell
b5   many things to many people and set them on the right track
with respect to the future, we would spin the story out by
saying things that are obvious to everyone. But it is worthwhile
adducing this point: that among the ancients, too, those who
gave things their names did not regard madness as shameful
c1   or a matter for reproach; for otherwise they would not have
connected this very word with the finest of the sciences, that by
which the future is judged, and named it the "manic" art. No,
they gave it this name thinking madness a fine thing when it
comes by divine dispensation; whereas people now crudely
c5   throw in the extra "t" and call it "mantic".[88] So too when the
ancients gave a name to the investigation sane men make into
the future by means of birds and the other signs they use, they
called it "oionoistic", because its proponents in a rational way
provide insight (*nous*) and information (*historia*) for human
d1   thinking (*oiêsis*); while moderns now call it "oiônistic", making
it more high-sounding with the long "o". So the ancients testify
to the fact that god-sent madness is a finer thing than man-made
sanity, by the very degree that mantic is a more perfect and
more valuable thing than oionistic, both when name is
d5   measured against name and when effect is measured against
effect. But again, in the case of the greatest maladies and sufferings that occur in certain families from some ancient causes
of divine anger, madness comes about in them and acts as
e1   interpreter, finding the necessary means of relief by recourse to
prayers and forms of service to the gods; as a result of which it
hits upon secret rites of purification and puts the man who is
touched by it[89] out of danger for both the present and the
future, so finding a release from his present evils for the one
245a who is rightly maddened and possessed. A third kind of possession and madness comes from the Muses:[90] taking a soft,
virgin soul and arousing it to a Bacchic frenzy of expression in
lyric and the other forms of poetry, it educates succeeding
a5   generations by glorifying myriad deeds of those of the past;
while the man who arrives at the doors of poetry without
madness from the Muses, convinced that after all expertise will
make him a good poet, both he and his poetry – the poetry of

the sane – are eclipsed by that of the mad, remaining imperfect and unfulfilled.

'All these and still more are the fine achievements I can relate   b1
to you of madness that comes from the gods. So let us have no fears about *that*, and let us not be alarmed by any argument that tries to frighten us into supposing that we should prefer the sane man as friend to the one who is disturbed; let it carry   b5
off the prize of victory only if it has shown this too – that love is not sent from the gods to help lover and beloved. We in our turn must prove the reverse, that such madness is given by the   c1
gods to allow us to achieve the greatest good fortune; and the proof will be disbelieved by the clever, believed by the wise.

'Well then: first, we must comprehend the truth about the nature of soul, both divine and human, by observing experiences and actions belonging to it; and the beginning of our   c5
proof is this:

'All soul is immortal. For that which is always in movement is immortal; that which moves something else, and is moved by something else, in ceasing from movement ceases from living. So only that which moves itself, because it does not abandon itself, never stops moving. But it is also source and first principle   c10
of movement for the other things which move. Now a first   d1
principle is something which does not come into being. For all that comes into being must come into being from a first principle, but a first principle itself cannot come into being from anything at all; for if a first principle came into being from anything, it would not do so from a first principle.[91] Since it is something that does not come into being, it must also be something which does not perish. For if a first principle is destroyed, neither will it   d5
ever come into being from anything itself nor will anything else come into being from it, given that all things must come into being from a first principle. It is in this way, then, that that which moves itself is a first principle of movement. It is not possible for this either to be destroyed or to come into being, or else the whole universe and the whole of that which comes   e1
to be might collapse together and come to a halt, and never again have a source from which things will be moved and come to be. And since that which is moved by itself has been shown

to be immortal, it will incur no shame to say that this is the
e5   essence and the definition of soul. For all body which has its
source of motion outside itself is soulless, whereas that which
has it within itself, from itself, is ensouled, this being the nature
of soul; and if this is the way it is – that that which moves
246a itself is nothing other than soul – then soul will necessarily be
something that neither comes into being nor dies.

'About its immortality, then, enough has been said. About
its form we must say the following: *that what kind of thing it
a5   is* belongs to a completely and utterly superhuman[92] exposition,
and a long one; to say *what it resembles* requires a lesser one,
one within human capacities. So let us speak in the latter way.
Let it then resemble the combined[93] power of a winged team of
horses and their charioteer. Now in the case of gods, horses
b1   and charioteers are all both good themselves and of good stock;
whereas in the case of the rest, there is a mixture. In the first
place, our driver[94] has charge of a pair; secondly, one of them
he finds noble and good, and of similar stock, while the other
is of the opposite stock, and opposite in its nature; so that the
b5   driving in our case is necessarily difficult and troublesome. How
it is, then, that some living creatures are called mortal and some
immortal, we must now try to say. All soul has the care of all
that is soulless, and ranges about the whole universe, coming
c1   to be now in one form, now in another. Now when it is perfectly
winged, it travels above the earth and governs the whole
cosmos; but the soul that has lost its wings is swept along until
it lays hold of something solid, where it settles down, taking on
an earthly body that seems to move itself because of the power
c5   of soul, and the whole is called a living creature, soul and body
fixed together, and acquires the name "mortal"; immortal it is
not, on the basis of any argument which has been reasoned
through, but because we have neither seen nor adequately con-
d1   ceived of a god, we imagine a kind of immortal living creature
which has a soul and has a body, and we imagine these combined for all time. But let this, and our account of it, be as is
pleasing to god;[95] let us grasp the cause of the loss of wings –
d5   why they fall from a soul. It is something like this.

'The natural property of a wing is to carry what is heavy

upwards, lifting it aloft to the region where the race of the gods
resides, and in a way,[96] of all the things belonging to the sphere
of the body, it has the greatest share in the divine, the divine   e1
being beautiful, wise, good and everything which is of that
kind;[97] so it is by these things that the plumage of the soul is
nourished and increased most of all, while the shameful, the
bad and in general the opposites of the other things make it
waste away and perish. First in the heavens travels Zeus, the   e5
great leader, driving a winged chariot, putting all things in
order and caring for all; after him there follows an army of
gods and divinities, ordered in eleven companies. For Hestia   247a
alone remains[98] in the house of the gods; of the rest, all those
who have their place among the number of the twelve take the
lead as commanders in the station given to each. Many, then,
and blessed are the paths to be seen along which the happy race   a5
of gods turns within the heavens, each of them performing what
belongs to him; and after them follows anyone who wishes and
is able to do so, for jealousy is excluded from the divine chorus.
But when they go to their feasting and to banquet, then they
travel to the summit of the arch of heaven, and the climb is   b1
steep: the chariots of the gods travel easily, being well balanced
and easily controlled, while the rest do so with difficulty; for
the horse that is partly bad weighs them down, inclining them
towards the earth through its weight, if any of the charioteers
has not trained him well. Here it is that the final labour,[99]   b5
the final contest, awaits a soul. Those souls that are called
immortal,[100] when they are at the top, travel outside and take
their stand upon the outer part of the heavens, and positioned   c1
like this they are carried round by its revolution, and gaze on
the things outside the heavens.

'Now the region above the heavens has never yet been celebrated as it deserves to be by any earthly poet, nor will it ever
be. But it is like this – for one must be bold enough to say what   c5
is true, especially when speaking about truth. This region is
occupied by being which really is, which is without colour or
shape, intangible, observable by the steersman of the soul alone,
by intellect, and to which the class of true knowledge relates.[101]   d1
Thus because the mind of a god is nourished by intellect and

knowledge unmixed, and so too that of every soul which is concerned to receive what is appropriate to it, it is glad at last to see what is and is nourished and made happy by gazing on

d5 what is true, until the revolution of the whole brings it around in a circle to the same point. In its circuit it sees justice itself, sees self-control,[102] sees knowledge – not that knowledge to which coming into being attaches, nor the knowledge that

e1 strangely differs in different items among the things that we now say are,[103] but that which is in what really is and which is really knowledge; and having feasted its gaze in the same way on the other things that really are, it descends back into the region within the heavens and goes home. When it arrives there,

e5 the charioteer stations his horses at their manger, throwing them ambrosia and giving them nectar to drink down with the ambrosia.[104]

248a   'This is the life of gods; of the other souls, the one that follows god best and has come to resemble him most raises the head of its charioteer into the region outside and is carried round with the revolution, meanwhile being disturbed by its

a5 horses and scarcely seeing the things that are; while another now rises, now sinks, and because of the force exerted by its horses sees some things but not others. The remaining souls follow after them, all straining to reach the place above but unable to do so, and are carried round together under the

b1 surface, trampling and jostling one another, each trying to get ahead of the next. So there ensues the greatest confusion among the sweating competitors, and in all of it, through their charioteers' incompetence, many souls are maimed, and many have their wings all broken; all of them with great labour depart

b5 without achieving a sight of what is, and afterwards feed on what only appears to nourish them.[105] The cause of their great eagerness to see the plain of truth where it lies is that the

c1 pasturage that is fitting for the best part of the soul[106] really comes from the meadow there, and that it is the nature of the wing that lifts up the soul to be nourished by this. And the ordinance of Destiny[107] is this: that whichever soul follows in the train of god and catches some sight of what is true shall

c5 remain free from sorrow until the next circuit, and if it is always

able to do this, it shall always remain free from harm; but whenever through inability to follow it fails to see, and through some mischance is weighed down by being filled with forgetfulness and incompetence, and because of the weight loses its wings and falls to the earth, then it is the law that this soul shall   d1
not be planted in any wild creature at its first birth;[108] rather, the one that saw most shall be planted in the seed of a man who will become a lover of wisdom, or of beauty, or devoted to the Muses and to love;[109] the second in the seed of a law-abiding king, or someone fit for generalship and ruling; the   d5
third in that of a man who devotes himself to the affairs of a city, or some expert in household or business affairs; the fourth in that of an exercise-loving trainer in the gymnasium, or of someone who will be concerned with healing the body; the fifth will have the life of a seer or of some expert in mystic rites; for   e1
the sixth, the fitting life will be that of a poet[110] or of some other type concerned with imitation; for the seventh that of a craftsman or farmer; for the eighth that of sophist or demagogue; for the ninth that of a tyrant. Among all these kinds, whoever lives justly receives a better portion, whoever lives   e5
unjustly receives a worse. For each soul only returns to the place from which it has come after ten thousand years;[111] it   249a
does not become winged before then, except in the case of the soul of the man who has lived the philosophical life without guile or who has united his love of boys with philosophy. These souls, with the third circuit of a thousand years, if they choose this life three times in succession, on that condition become winged and depart, in the three-thousandth year. But the rest,   a5
when they finish their first life, undergo judgement, and after judgement some of them go to the places of correction under the earth and pay their penalty, while others are lifted up by Justice into some region of the heavens and live a life of a kind merited by their life in human form.[112] In the thousandth year,   b1
both sorts come to an allotment and choice[113] of their second life, and each chooses whichever it wishes: then a human soul passes even into the life of a wild animal, and what was once a   b5
man back into a man from a wild animal. For the soul which has never seen the truth shall not enter this shape of ours. A

human being must comprehend what is said universally, arising
from many sensations and being collected together into one
through reasoning; and this is a recollection[114] of those things
which our soul once saw when it travelled in company with
god and treated with contempt the things we now say are,[115]
and when it poked its head up into what really is. Hence it is
with justice that only the thought of the philosopher becomes
winged; for so far as it can it is close, through memory, to those
things his closeness to which gives a god his divinity. Thus if a
man uses such reminders[116] rightly, being continually initiated
in perfect rites, he alone achieves real perfection;[117] and standing
aside from human concerns, and coming close to the divine,
he is admonished by the many for being disturbed, when his
real state is one of possession, which goes unrecognized by
the many.

'Well then, this is the outcome of my whole account of the
fourth kind of madness – the madness of the man who, on
seeing beauty here on earth, and being reminded of true beauty,
becomes winged and, fluttering with eagerness to fly upwards
but unable to leave the ground, looking upwards like a bird,
and taking no heed of the things below, causes him to be
regarded as mad:[118] the outcome is that this in fact reveals itself
as the best of all the kinds of divine possession and from the
best of sources for the man who is subject to it and shares in it,
and that it is when he partakes in this madness that the man
who loves the beautiful[119] is called a lover. For as has been said,
every soul of a human being has by the law of its nature
observed the things that are, or else it would not have entered
this creature, man; but it is not easy for every soul to gain from
things here a recollection of those other things, either for those
which only briefly saw the things there at that earlier time, or
for those which fall to earth and have the misfortune to be
turned to injustice by keeping certain kinds of company, forget-
ting the holy things they saw then. Few souls are left who have
sufficient memory; and these, when they see some likeness of
the things there, are driven out of their wits with amazement
and lose control of themselves, though they do not know what
has happened to them because they cannot properly see through

it. Now in the earthly likenesses of justice and self-control and the other things that are of value to souls, there is no illumination, but through dulled organs just a few individuals approach their images and with difficulty observe the nature of what is   b5
imaged in them; but in that earlier time beauty was there to see, blazing out, when with a happy company – ourselves[120] following with Zeus, others with different gods – they *saw* a blessed sight there before them, and were initiated into what it is right to call most blessed of rites, which we celebrated, whole   c1
in ourselves, and untouched by the evils that awaited us in a later time, with our gaze turned in our final initiation towards whole, simple, unchanging and blissful revelations, in a pure light, pure ourselves and not entombed in this thing which we   c5
now carry round with us and call body, imprisoned like oysters.

'Let this, then, be our concession to memory, which has made me speak now at some length out of longing for what was before;[121] but on the subject of beauty – as we said, it shone out   d1
when in company with those other things, and now that we have come to earth we have found it gleaming most clearly through the clearest of the senses that we have. For of all the sensations coming to us through the body, sight is the keenest: wisdom we do not see with it – the feelings of love it would   d5
cause in us would be terrible, if it allowed some such clear image of itself to reach our sight, and so too with the other objects of love;[122] but as it is, beauty alone has acquired this privilege, of being most evident and most loved. Thus the man   e1
whose initiation was not recent, or who has been corrupted, does not move keenly from here to there, to beauty itself, when he gazes on its namesake here, so that he does not revere it when he looks at it but, surrendering himself to pleasure, does his best to go on four feet like an animal and father offspring   e5
and, keeping close company with excess,[123] has no fear or shame   251a
in pursuing pleasure contrary to nature; while the newly initiated, the man who observed much of what was visible to him before, whenever he sees a godlike face or some form of body which imitates beauty well, first shudders, feeling something of the fears he had before, then reveres what he sees like   a5
a god as he gazes at it and, if he were not afraid of appearing

thoroughly mad, would sacrifice to his beloved as if to a statue
of a god. When he has seen him, the expected change comes
over him following the shuddering – sweating and a high fever;
for he is warmed by receiving the effluence of beauty that is the
natural nourishment of his plumage, and with that warming
there is a melting of the parts around its base, which have
long since become hard and closed up, so preventing it from
sprouting, and with the incoming stream of nourishment the
quills of the feathers swell and set to growing from their roots
under the surface of the whole form of the soul; for formerly
the whole of it was winged. Meanwhile all of it throbs and
palpitates, and the experience is like that of cutting teeth, the
itching and the aching that occur around the gums when the
teeth are just coming through: such is the state of the soul of
the man who is beginning to sprout wings – it throbs and aches
and tickles as it grows its feathers. So when it gazes at the boy's
beauty, and is nourished and warmed by receiving particles
(*merê*) which come to it (*epionta*) in a flood (*rheonta*) from there
(hence, of course, the name we give them, desire (*himeros*)[124]), it
experiences relief from its anguish and is filled with joy; but
when it is apart and becomes parched, the openings of the
passages through which the feathers push their way out are
dried up and closed, so shutting off their shoots, and these, shut
in with the desire,[125] throb like pulsing arteries, each of them
pricking at the outlet corresponding to it, so that the entire
soul, stung all over, goes mad with pain; but then, remembering
the boy with his beauty,[126] it rejoices again. The mixture of
both these states makes it despair at the strangeness of its
condition, raging in its perplexity, and in its madness it can
neither sleep at night nor keep still where it is by day, but in its
yearning runs to wherever it thinks it will see the possessor of
the beauty it longs for; and, when it has seen him and channelled
desire[127] in to itself, it releases what was pent up before, and,
finding a breathing space, it ceases from its stinging birth-pains,
once more enjoying this for the moment as the sweetest pleasure. This it does not willingly give up, nor does it value anyone
above the one with beauty, but quite forgets mother, brothers,
friends, all together, loses wealth through neglect without

caring a jot about it, and, feeling contempt for all the accepted   a5
standards of propriety and good taste in which it previously
prided itself, it is ready to act the part of a slave and sleep
wherever it is allowed to do so, provided it is as close as possible
to the object of its yearning; for in addition to its reverence for
the one who possesses the beauty, it has found him to be the   b1
sole healer of its greatest labours. This experience, my beautiful
boy, the one to whom my speech is addressed, men term love;
but when you hear what gods call it I expect you will laugh,
because of your youth. I think some Homeric experts cite two   b5
verses to Love from the less well-known poems, the second of
which is quite outrageous and not very metrical; they celebrate
him like this:

We mortals call him Mighty Love, a wingèd power of great renown,
Immortals call him Fledgeling Dove – since Eros' wings lack down.[128]

You may believe this or you may not; but at any rate the cause   c1
of the lover's experience and the experience itself are as I have
described.

'If the man who is taken by Love belongs among the followers
of Zeus, he is able to bear the burden of the Feathery One with
some sedateness; but as for those who were attendants of Ares[129]   c5
and made the circuit with him, when they are captured by Love
and think that they are being wronged in some way by the one
they love, they become murderous and ready to sacrifice both
themselves and their beloved. Just so each lives after the pattern   d1
of the god in whose chorus he was, honouring him by imitating
him in his life so far as he can, provided that he is uncorrupted
and living out the life following his first birth here on earth;
and he behaves in this way in his associations both with those
he loves and with everyone else. So each selects his love from   d5
the ranks of the beautiful according to his own disposition and,
as if that love were the very god he followed, fashions and
adorns him like a statue for himself, in order to honour him   e1
and celebrate his mystic rites. Thus those who belong to Zeus
seek that the one loved by themselves should be Zeus-like in
respect of his soul; so they look to see whether he is naturally

disposed towards philosophy and leadership, and when they
have found him and fallen in love, they do everything to make
e5 him like this. So if they haven't embarked on this practice[130] before now, now they do undertake it, both learning from wherever
they can and finding out for themselves; and as they follow the
253a scent from within themselves to the discovery of the nature of
their own god, they find the means to it through the compulsion
on them to gaze intensely on the god, and grasping him through
memory, and possessed by him, it is from him that they take
their habits and ways, to the extent that it is possible for man
a5 to share in god; and because they count their beloved responsible for these very things, they love him even more, and if it is
from Zeus that they draw, like Bacchants, they pour the draught
b1 over the soul of their loved one and make him as like their god
as possible. As for those who followed with Hera, they seek
someone regal in nature, and when they have found him they
do all the same things in respect of him. Those who belong to
Apollo and each of the other gods proceed in the same way in
accordance with their god and seek that their boy should be of
b5 the same nature; and when they acquire him, imitating the god
themselves and persuading and disciplining their beloved, they
draw him into the way of life and pattern of the god, to the
extent that each is able, without showing jealousy or mean
c1 ill-will towards their beloved; rather, they act as they do because
they are trying as much as they can, in every way, to draw him
into complete resemblance to themselves and to whichever god
they honour. The eagerness of those who are truly in love, then,
and its outcome[131] – if, that is, they manage to achieve what
they eagerly desire in the way I have said – are thus rendered
c5 beautiful and bring happiness from the friend who is maddened
through love to the object of his affection, if he is caught; and
one who is caught is captured in the following way.

'Just as at the beginning of this story we divided each soul
into three forms,[132] two like horses and the third with the role
d1 of charioteer, let this still stand now. Of the horses, one, we
say, is good, the other not; but we did not describe what the
excellence of the good horse was, or the badness of the bad
horse, and now we must. Well then, the first of the two, which

is on the nobler station,[133] is erect in form and clean-limbed,   d5
high-necked, nose somewhat hooked, white in colour, with
black eyes, a lover of honour when joined with restraint and a
sense of shame, and a companion of true glory, needing no
whip, responding to spoken orders[134] alone; the other is crooked   e1
in shape, gross, a random collection of parts, with a short,
powerful neck, flat-nosed, black-skinned, grey-eyed, bloodshot,
companion of excess[135] and boastfulness, shaggy around the
ears, deaf, hardly yielding to whip and goad together. Now   e5
when the charioteer first catches sight of the light of his love,
warms the whole soul with the seeing of it, and begins to be
filled with tickling and pricks of longing, the horse that is   254a
obedient to the charioteer, constrained then as always by
shame, holds itself back from leaping on the loved one; while
the other no longer takes any heed of goading or the whip from
the charioteer but springs powerfully forward and, causing all   a5
kinds of trouble to his yoke-mate and the charioteer, forces
them to move towards the beloved and mention to him the
delights of sex. At the start, the two of them resist, indignant   b1
at the idea of being forced to do terrible and improper things;
but finally, when there is no limit to the trouble it causes, they
follow its lead, giving in and agreeing to do what it tells them
to do. And now they are close to the beloved, and they see the
beloved's face, flashing like lightning. As the charioteer sees it,   b5
his memory is carried back to the nature of beauty and again
sees it standing together with self-control on a holy pedestal; at
the sight it becomes frightened, and in sudden reverence falls
on its back, and is forced at the same time to pull back the reins   c1
so violently as to bring both horses down on their haunches,
the one willingly, because of its lack of resistance to him, but
the horse of excess[136] much against its will. When they have
backed off a little way, the first horse drenches the whole soul   c5
with sweat from shame and alarm, while the other, when it has
recovered from the pain caused to it by the bit and its fall,
scarcely gets its breath back before it breaks into angry abuse,
repeatedly reviling the charioteer and its yoke-mate for cow-
ardly and unmanly desertion of their agreed position; and again   d1
it tries to compel them to approach, unwilling as they are, and

barely concedes when they beg him to postpone it until a later
time. When the agreed time comes, and they pretend not to
d5 remember, it reminds them; struggling, neighing, pulling, it
forces them to approach the beloved again to make the same
proposition, and as soon as they are close to him, head down
and tail outstretched, teeth clamped on its bit, it pulls shame-
e1 lessly; but the same thing happens to the charioteer as before,
only even more violently, as he falls back as if from a starting-
barrier;[137] still more violently, he wrenches the bit back and
forces it from the teeth of the horse of excess, spattering its
evil-speaking tongue and its jaws with blood and, thrusting its
e5 legs and haunches to the ground, 'gives it over to pains'.[138]
When the bad horse has had the same thing happen to it repeatedly and it ceases from its excess, now humbled it allows the
charioteer with his foresight to lead, and when it sees the boy
in his beauty, it nearly dies of fright; and the result is that then
255a the soul of the lover follows the beloved in reverence and awe.
So because he receives every kind of service, as if equal to the
gods, from a lover who is not pretending to be in love but
genuinely in this state, and because he naturally feels friendship
for the man who renders him service, even if perhaps in the
a5 past he has been prejudiced against him by hearing his schoolfel-
lows or others say that it is shameful to associate with a lover,
and repulses the one in love for that reason, as time goes on he
b1 is led both by his age, and by necessity, towards admitting him
to his company; for it is surely against fate that bad be friend
to bad, or that good not be friend to good. Once he has admitted
him, and accepted his conversation and his company, the goodwill that he experiences at close quarters from the one in love
b5 astounds the beloved, as he clearly sees that not even all his
other friends and his relations together have anything to offer
by way of friendship in comparison with the friend who is
divinely possessed. And when he continues doing this, and
association is combined with physical contact in the gymnasium
c1 and on the other occasions when people come together, then it
is that the springs of that stream which Zeus when in love with
Ganymede named 'desire'[139] flow in abundance upon the lover,
some sinking within him and some flowing off outside him as

he brims over; and as a breath of wind or some echo rebounds
from smooth, hard surfaces and returns to the source from   c5
which it issued, so the stream of beauty passes back into its
possessor[140] through his eyes, which is its natural route to the
soul; arriving there and setting him all aflutter, it waters the   d1
passages of the feathers and causes the wings to grow, and fills
the soul of the loved one in his turn with love. So he is in love,
but as to what he is in love with, he is at a loss; and he neither
knows what has happened to him nor can he even begin to
express what it is, but – like a man who has caught eye-disease   d5
from someone – he can give no account of it and is unaware
that he is seeing himself in the one who loves as if in a mirror.
And when his lover is with him, like him he ceases from his
anguish; when he is absent, again like him he longs and is
longed for, because he is feeling love back, an image of the   e1
lover's love, though he calls what he has and thinks of it not as
love but as friendship.[141] His desire is similar to his lover's but
weaker: to see, touch, kiss and lie down together; and indeed,
as one might expect, soon afterwards he does just that. So as   e5
they lie together, the lover's licentious horse has something to
say to the charioteer and claims the right to a little enjoyment   256a
as recompense for many labours endured; while its counterpart
in the beloved has nothing to say, but, swelling with confused
passion, it embraces the lover and kisses him, welcoming him
as someone full of goodwill, and when they lie down together,
it is ready not to refuse to do its own part in granting favours   a5
to the one in love, should he beg to receive them; but its yoke-
fellow, for its part, together with the charioteer, resists this with
a reasoned sense of shame. And then, well, if the better elements
of their minds get the upper hand by drawing them to a well-
ordered life, and to philosophy, they pass their life here in   b1
blessedness and harmony, masters of themselves and orderly
in their behaviour, having enslaved that part through which
badness attempted to enter the soul and having freed that
part through which goodness enters; and when they die they
become winged and light, and have won one of their three   b5
submissions[142] in these, the true Olympic games – and neither
human sanity nor divine madness has any greater good to offer

c1 a man than this. But if they live a coarser way of life, devoted
not to wisdom but to honour, then perhaps, I suppose, when
they are drinking or in some other moment of carelessness, the
licentious horses in the two of them catch them off their guard,
bring them together and make that choice which is called
c5 blessed by the many, and carry it through; and, once having
done so, they continue with that choice, but sparingly, because
what they are doing has not been approved by their whole
mind. So these too spend their lives as mutual friends, though
d1 not to the same degree as the other pair, both during the course
of their love and when they have passed beyond it, believing
that they have given and received the most binding pledges,
which it would be against piety to break by ever becoming
d5 enemies. On their death they leave the body without wings but
with the impulse to gain them, so that they carry off no small
reward for their lovers' madness; for it is ordained that those
who have already begun on the journey under the heavens shall
no longer pass into the darkness of the journey under the earth
e1 but shall rather live in the light and be happy as they travel
with each other, and acquire matching plumage, when they
acquire it, because of their love.

'These are the blessings, my boy, so great as to be counted
divine, that will come to you from the friendship of a lover, in
the way I have described; whereas the acquaintance of the one
e5 not in love, which is diluted with a merely mortal good sense,
dispensing miserly benefits of a mortal kind, engenders in the
soul that is the object of its attachment a meanness that, though
257a praised by the many as a virtue, will cause it to wallow mind-
lessly around the earth and under the earth for nine thousand
years.'

This, dear god of love, is offered and paid to you as the finest
a5 and best palinode of which I am capable, especially given that
it was forced to use somewhat poetical language because of
Phaedrus.[143] Forgive what went before and regard this with
favour; be kind and gracious – do not in anger take away or
maim the expertise in love that you gave me,[144] and grant that
b1 I be valued still more than now by the beautiful. If in our earlier
speech Phaedrus and I said anything harsh against you, blame

Lysias as the instigator of the speech, and make him cease
from speeches of that kind, turning him instead, as his brother
Polemarchus[145] has been turned, to philosophy, so that his lover
here too may no longer waver, as he does now, between the   b5
two choices but may single-mindedly direct his life towards
love accompanied by talk[146] of a philosophical kind.

PHAEDRUS I pray with you, Socrates: if indeed that is better   c1
for us, that may we have. But as for your speech, for some time
I have been amazed at how much finer you managed to make
it than the one before; so that I have a suspicion Lysias will
appear wretched to me in comparison, if he really does consent
to put up another in competition with it. Indeed, my amazing
friend, just recently one of the politicians was using this very   c5
reproach to abuse him, and all through the abuse kept calling
him a 'speech-writer'; so perhaps we shall find him refraining
from writing out of concern for his reputation.

SOCRATES An absurd idea, young man; you much mistake your   d1
friend, if you think him so frightened of mere noise. But perhaps
you think that the man who was abusing him really meant what
he said.

PHAEDRUS He seemed to, Socrates; and I think you know   d5
yourself that the men with the most power and dignity in our
cities are ashamed to write speeches and leave compositions of
theirs behind them, for fear of what posterity will think of them
– they're afraid they'll be called sophists.

SOCRATES Phaedrus, you don't know the expression 'pleasant
bend';[147] and besides the bend you're missing the point that the
politicians who have the highest opinion of themselves are
most in love with speech-writing and with leaving compositions
behind them, to judge at any rate from the fact that whenever
they write a speech, they are so pleased with those who com-   e5
mend it that they add in at the beginning the names of those
who commend them on each occasion.

PHAEDRUS What do you mean by that? I don't understand.

SOCRATES You don't understand that at the beginning of a   258a
politician's composition the commender's name is written first?

PHAEDRUS How so?

SOCRATES The writer says, I think, 'It was resolved by the

a5   council,' or 'by the people' or both, and 'So-and-so said', referring to his own dear self with great pomposity and self-eulogy;
then he proceeds with what he has to say, demonstrating his
own wisdom to those commending him, sometimes making a
very long composition of it; or does such a thing seem to you
to be anything other than a written speech?

b1   PHAEDRUS Not to me.

SOCRATES Then if it stays written down, the author[148] leaves
the theatre delighted; but if it is rubbed out and he loses his
chance of being a speech-writer and of being recognized as a
b5   writer, he and his friends go into mourning.

PHAEDRUS Very much so.

SOCRATES And clearly they behave like this not because they
despise the profession, but because they regard it with
admiration.

PHAEDRUS Yes indeed.

b10   SOCRATES Well then: when a person becomes a good enough
c1   orator or king to acquire the capacity of a Lycurgus, a Solon
or a Darius[149] and achieve immortality as a speech-writer in a
city, doesn't he think himself equal to the gods even while he is
alive, and don't those who come later think the very same of
c5   him, when they observe his compositions?

PHAEDRUS Very much so.

SOCRATES So do you think anyone of that kind, whoever he is
and however ill disposed towards Lysias, reproaches him on
this count – that he is a writer?

c10   PHAEDRUS It's not very likely, from what you say; if he did, it
seems he would be reproaching what he himself desires.

d1   SOCRATES This much, then, is clear to everyone, that writing
speeches is not *itself* something shameful.

PHAEDRUS How could it be?

SOCRATES But what *is* shameful, I think, is speaking and writ-
d5   ing and doing it not well but shamefully and badly.

PHAEDRUS Clearly.

SOCRATES So what is the way to write well or badly? Do we
need, Phaedrus, to examine Lysias, perhaps, on this subject, and
anyone else who has so far written anything, or will write any-
d10   thing, whether it's a political composition or a private one, and

whether he writes it as a poet, in verse, or in plain man's prose?

PHAEDRUS You really ask if we need to? What would anyone ei
live for, if I may put it as strongly as that, if not for such
pleasures as this? Not, I think, for those which have to be
preceded by pain if one is to enjoy pleasure at all – a feature
possessed by nearly all the pleasures relating to the body; which
is why in fact they are called slavish, and justly so.[150] e5

SOCRATES We have plenty of time, it seems; and there's something else: I think that as the cicadas sing above our heads in
their usual fashion in the heat, and converse with[151] each other, 259a
they are also watching us. So if they saw us behaving like most
people at midday, and not conversing but nodding off under
their spell through lazy-mindedness, they would justly laugh at
us, thinking that some slaves had come to their gathering-place a5
and were having their midday sleep around the spring, like
sheep; but if they see us conversing and sailing past them unbe-
witched by their Siren song, perhaps they may respect us and b1
give us that gift which they have from the gods to give to men.

PHAEDRUS What is this gift they have? I don't seem to have
heard of it.

SOCRATES A man who loves the Muses really ought to have b5
heard of things like this. The story is that these creatures were
once human beings, belonging to a time before the Muses were
born, and that with the birth of the Muses and the appearance
of song some of the people of the time were so unhinged by
pleasure that in their singing they neglected to eat and drink, c1
and failed to notice that they had died. From them the race of
cicadas later sprang, with this gift from the Muses, that from
their birth they have no need of sustenance but immediately
start singing, with no food and no drink, and sing until they c5
die; then they go and report to the Muses which among those
here honours which of them. To Terpsichore they report those
who have honoured her in the choral dance, and so make them d1
dearer to her; to Erato those who have honoured her in the
affairs of love; and to the other Muses similarly, according to
the form of honour belonging to each; but to Calliope, the
eldest, and to Ourania, who comes after her, they announce
those who spend their time in philosophy and honour the music d5

that belongs to the two of them – who, most of all the Muses, are concerned both with the heavens and with speech,[152] both divine and human, and whose voices carry most beautifully. So there are many reasons why we should say something and not sleep in the midday heat.

PHAEDRUS Yes, we should.

e1 SOCRATES Then we should consider what we proposed just now: speeches – in what way they will be well said and written, and in what way they will not.

PHAEDRUS Clearly.

SOCRATES Well then, for things that are going to be said *well*, and beautifully, mustn't there be knowledge in the mind of the speaker of the truth about whatever he means to speak of?

PHAEDRUS What I have heard about this, my dear Socrates, is 260a that there is no necessity for the man who means to be an orator to understand what is really just but only what would appear so to the majority of those who will give judgement; and not what is really good or beautiful but whatever will appear so; because persuasion comes from that and not from the truth.

a5 SOCRATES Whatever wise people say, Phaedrus, is 'a word not to be cast aside',[153] and we should always look to see whether they may not be right; what you just said, particularly, must not be dismissed.

PHAEDRUS Quite right.

SOCRATES Let us consider it like this.

PHAEDRUS How?

b1 SOCRATES If I were persuading you to defend yourself against the enemy by getting a horse, and neither of us knew what a horse was, but I happened to know just so much about you, that Phaedrus thinks a horse is that tame animal which has the largest ears –

b5 PHAEDRUS It would be ridiculous, Socrates.

SOCRATES Not so ridiculous yet; but it would be when I tried in earnest to persuade you by putting together a speech in praise of the donkey, labelling it a horse and saying that the beast would be an invaluable acquisition both at home and on active c1 service, useful to fight from and capable too of carrying baggage, and good for many other purposes.

PHAEDRUS Then it would be thoroughly ridiculous.

SOCRATES Well then, isn't it better to be ridiculous and a friend than to be clever and an enemy?

PHAEDRUS It seems so.   c5

SOCRATES So when an expert in rhetoric who is ignorant of good and bad finds a city in the same condition and tries to persuade it, by making his eulogy not about a miserable donkey as if it were a horse but about what is bad as if it were good, and – having applied himself to what the masses think – actually persuades the city to do something bad instead of good, what   c10 sort of harvest do you think rhetoric reaps after that from the   d1 seed it sowed?

PHAEDRUS Not a very good one.

SOCRATES Well, my good friend, have we abused the science of speaking more coarsely than we should? She might perhaps say 'What nonsense is this you're talking, you fine people?   d5 I don't insist that anyone who learns how to speak should be ignorant of the truth; on the contrary, if I advise anything, it is that he should acquire the truth first and then get hold of me. But this at any rate is my boast, that without me the man who knows what is true will be quite unable to persuade scientifically.'

PHAEDRUS So will she be right in saying this?   e1

SOCRATES I say she will; if, that is, the arguments[154] advancing on her testify that she is a science. For it seems to me as if I am hearing certain arguments approaching and solemnly protesting even before the case comes to court that she is lying, and is not a science but an unscientific knack; without a grasp of truth,   e5 saith the Laconian,[155] a genuine science of speaking neither exists nor will come into existence in the future.

PHAEDRUS We need these arguments, Socrates; bring them   261a here before us and examine what they say and how they say it.

SOCRATES Come here then, you noble beasts, and persuade Phaedrus of the beautiful offspring[156] that unless he engages in philosophy sufficiently well, neither will he ever be a sufficiently   a5 good speaker about anything. Let Phaedrus answer you.

PHAEDRUS (addressing the Arguments) Ask your questions.

SOCRATES/ARGUMENTS Well then, will not the science of

rhetoric as a whole be a kind of leading of the soul by means of speech,[157] not only in law-courts and other kinds of public gatherings but in private ones too – the same science, whether
b1 it is concerned with small matters or large ones, and something which possesses no more value, if properly understood, when it comes into play in relation to things of importance than when it does with things of no importance? Is this what you've heard about it?

PHAEDRUS Zeus! No, not quite that, I must say. A science of
b5 speaking and writing is perhaps especially employed in lawsuits, though scientific speaking is also involved in public addresses; I have not heard of any extension of it beyond that.

SOCRATES/ARGUMENTS What? Have you only heard of the manuals on rhetoric by Nestor and Odysseus, the ones they composed at Troy when they had nothing to do? You haven't heard of those of Palamedes?[158]

c1 PHAEDRUS Neither – Zeus! – have I heard of Nestor's, unless you're dressing up Gorgias as a kind of Nestor, or maybe a Thrasymachus or Theodorus as Odysseus.[159]

SOCRATES/ARGUMENTS Perhaps. But anyway let them pass.
c5 Now you tell us this: What do opposing parties in law-courts do? Don't they give opposing speeches? Or what shall we say?

PHAEDRUS Just that.

SOCRATES/ARGUMENTS About the just and unjust?

PHAEDRUS Yes.

c10 SOCRATES/ARGUMENTS So the man who does this scientifically
d1 will make the same thing appear to the same people at one time just and, whenever he wishes, unjust?

PHAEDRUS Of course.

SOCRATES/ARGUMENTS And in public addresses he will make the same things seem to the city at one time good, at another the opposite?[160]

d5 PHAEDRUS Just so.

SOCRATES/ARGUMENTS Well, don't we recognize the Eleatic Palamedes as speaking scientifically so as to make the same things appear to his hearers to be like and unlike, one and many, at rest and in motion?[161]

PHAEDRUS Yes indeed.

SOCRATES/ARGUMENTS Then the science of giving opposing   d10
speeches is not restricted to law-courts and public addresses,   e1
but, it seems, there will be this single science – if indeed it *is* a
science – in relation to everything that is said: the science that
enables one to make everything which is capable of being made
to resemble something else resemble everything which it is
capable of being made to resemble, and to bring it to light when
someone else makes one thing resemble another and tries to
disguise it.

PHAEDRUS What sort of thing do you mean?   e5

SOCRATES/ARGUMENTS I think it will become clear if we direct
our search this way: Does deception occur more in the case of
things that are widely different or in those that differ little?

PHAEDRUS In those that differ little.   262a

SOCRATES/ARGUMENTS At any rate, when you are passing over
from one thing to its opposite you will be more likely to escape
detection if you take small steps than if you take large ones.

PHAEDRUS Certainly.

SOCRATES/ARGUMENTS In that case the person who means to   a5
deceive someone else, but be undeceived himself, must have a
precise knowledge of the likeness and unlikeness of the things
that are.[162]

PHAEDRUS Yes, necessarily.

SOCRATES/ARGUMENTS So will he be able, if he is ignorant of
the truth of each thing, to identify the likeness, whether small or   a10
great, that the other things have to the thing he does not know?

PHAEDRUS Impossible.   b1

SOCRATES/ARGUMENTS Then clearly those who hold beliefs
contrary to what is the case and are deceived have this kind of
thing creeping in on them through certain likenesses.

PHAEDRUS It does happen that way.

SOCRATES/ARGUMENTS So is there any way in which a man   b5
will be a scientific expert at making others cross over little by
little from what is the case on each occasion, via the likenesses,
leading them off towards the opposite, or at escaping this himself, if he has not recognized what each of the things that are
actually is?

PHAEDRUS No, never.

CI SOCRATES/ARGUMENTS In that case, my friend, anyone who does not know the truth, but has made it his business to hunt down appearances, will give us a science of speech that will, so it seems, be ridiculously unscientific.

PHAEDRUS You may be right.

C5 SOCRATES (*returning to his own persona*) So do you want to take the speech of Lysias you're carrying, and the ones you and I made,[163] and see in them something of the features we say are scientific and unscientific?

PHAEDRUS Yes, I think so, more than anything; as things are, our discussion is somewhat bare, because we do not have sufficient examples.

C10 SOCRATES What's more, by some chance, it seems, the pair of
D1 speeches[164] as they were given do have in them an example of a sort of how someone who knows the truth can mislead his audience by playing with them.[165] I myself, Phaedrus, blame the gods of the place; and perhaps too the spokesmen of the Muses
D5 who sing over our heads may have breathed this gift upon us – for I don't think *I* share in any science of speaking.

PHAEDRUS So be it; only make clear what you're saying.

SOCRATES Well, read me the beginning of Lysias' speech.

E1 PHAEDRUS 'How it is with me, you know, and how I think it is to our advantage that these things should happen, you have heard me say; and I claim that I should not fail to achieve the things I ask for because I happen not to be in love with you. Those in love repent of whatever services they do at the point –'

E5 SOCRATES Stop! We need to say, then, where the author goes wrong and what he does unscientifically – am I right?

263a PHAEDRUS Yes.

SOCRATES Isn't this sort of thing, at least, clear to anyone: that we're of one mind about some things like this, and at odds about others?

A5 PHAEDRUS I think I understand what you mean, but tell me still more clearly.

SOCRATES When someone utters the name of iron, or of silver, don't we all have the same thing in mind?

PHAEDRUS Absolutely.

SOCRATES What about the names of just, or good?[166] Doesn't

one of us go off in one direction, another in another, so that   a10
we disagree both with each other and with ourselves?

PHAEDRUS We certainly do.

SOCRATES Then we are in accord in some cases, not in others.   b1

PHAEDRUS Just so.

SOCRATES So in which of the two cases are we easier to deceive,
and in which does rhetoric have the greater power?

PHAEDRUS Clearly in those cases where we go off in different   b5
directions.

SOCRATES So the one who means to pursue a science of rhetoric
must first have divided these up methodically and grasped some
mark which distinguishes each of the two kinds, those in which
most people[167] are bound to tread uncertainly, and those in
which they are not.

PHAEDRUS A fine kind of thing he will have identified, Socrates,   c1
if he grasps this!

SOCRATES Then, I think, as he comes across each thing, he
must not be caught unawares but look sharply to see which of
the two types the thing he is going to speak about belongs to.   c5

PHAEDRUS Right.

SOCRATES Well then, are we to say that *love* belongs with the
disputed cases or the undisputed ones?

PHAEDRUS With the disputed, surely; otherwise, do you think
it would have been possible for you to say what you said about   c10
it just now, both that it is harmful to beloved and lover, and
then on the other hand that it is really the greatest of goods?

SOCRATES Admirably said; but tell me this too – for of course   d1
because of my inspired condition then, I don't quite remember
– whether I defined love when beginning my speech.

PHAEDRUS Zeus! Yes, indeed you did, most emphatically.

SOCRATES Dear me! How much more scientific you're saying   d5
the Nymphs, daughters of Achelous, and Pan, son of Hermes,
are than Lysias, son of Cephalus, in the business of speaking!
Or am I wrong? Did Lysias too compel us when beginning his
speech on love to take love as one definite thing that he himself   e1
had in mind, and did he then bring the whole speech that
followed to its conclusion by ordering it in relation to that?
Shall we read the beginning again?

PHAEDRUS If you think we should; but what you're looking for isn't there.

e5 SOCRATES Quote it, so I can hear it from the man himself.

PHAEDRUS 'How it is with me, you know, and how I think it is to our advantage that these things should happen, you have
264a heard me say; and I claim that I should not fail to achieve the things I ask for because I happen not to be in love with you. Those in love repent of whatever services they do at the point they cease from their desire –'

SOCRATES He does indeed seem to be a long way from doing
a5 what we're looking for, since he doesn't even begin at the beginning but from the end, trying to swim through his speech in reverse, on his back, and begins from the things the lover would say to his beloved when he'd already finished loving. Or am I wrong, Phaedrus, dear thing?[168]

b1 PHAEDRUS What he makes his speech about, Socrates, is certainly an ending.[169]

SOCRATES What about the rest? Don't the elements of the speech seem to have been thrown in a random heap? Or do you
b5 think the second thing he said had to be placed second for some essential reason, or any of the others where *they* were? It seemed to me, as one who knows nothing about it, that the writer had said just what happened to occur to him, in a not ignoble way; but do you know of any constraint deriving from the science of speech-writing which made him place these thoughts one beside another in this order?

PHAEDRUS You're kind to think me competent to understand
c1 so precisely what he has done.

SOCRATES But this much I think you would say: that every speech should be put together like a living creature, as it were with a body of its own, so as not to lack either a head or feet
c5 but to have both middle parts and extremities, so written as to fit both each other and the whole.

PHAEDRUS Yes indeed.

SOCRATES Well then, ask if your friend's speech is like this or if it's some other way, and you'll find it exactly like the epigram that some say is inscribed on the tomb of Midas the Phrygian.[170]

PHAEDRUS What's this epigram, and what feature of it are you   d1
talking about?

SOCRATES The poem's this:

> A bronze-clad maid, I stand on Midas' tomb,
> As long as rivers run and trees grow tall,
> A guardian of this much-lamented grave,   d5
> I'll tell the traveller: Midas rests within.

I think you see that it makes no difference whether any part of   e1
it is put first or last.

PHAEDRUS You're making fun of our speech, Socrates.

SOCRATES Well, to avoid your becoming upset, let's leave this
speech to one side – though it does seem to me to contain plenty   e5
of examples which someone could glance at with profit, if not
exactly by trying to imitate them – and pass on to the others.
For in my view there was something in them which should be
noticed by those who wish to enquire into speeches.

PHAEDRUS What sort of thing do you mean?   265a

SOCRATES They were, I think, opposites: one of them said that
favours should be granted to the one in love, the other to the
one not.

PHAEDRUS And very manfully too.

SOCRATES I thought you were going to speak the truth, and   a5
say 'madly', which in fact was the very thing I was looking for.
We said, didn't we, that love was a kind of madness?

PHAEDRUS Yes.

SOCRATES And that there were two kinds of madness, the one
caused by sicknesses of a human sort, the other coming about   a10
from a divinely caused reversal of our customary ways of
behaving?

PHAEDRUS Certainly.   b1

SOCRATES And of the divine kind we distinguished four parts,
belonging to four gods, taking the madness of the seer as
Apollo's inspiration, that of mystic rites as Dionysus', poetic
madness, for its part, as the Muses', and the fourth as that
belonging to Aphrodite and Love. The madness of love we said   b5

was best, and – by expressing the experience of love through some kind of simile, which allowed us perhaps to grasp some truth, though maybe also it took us in a wrong direction, and
c1 mixing together a not wholly implausible speech – we sang a playful hymn in the form of a story, in a fittingly quiet way, to my master and yours, Phaedrus, Love, watcher over beautiful boys.

PHAEDRUS And it gave me great pleasure to hear it.
c5 SOCRATES Well then, let's take up this point from it: how the speech[171] was able to pass over from censure to praise.

PHAEDRUS Precisely what aspect are you referring to?

SOCRATES To me it seems that the rest really was playfully done, by way of amusement; but by chance two kinds of thing[172] found expression, whose significance it would be gratifying to grasp in a scientific way.

PHAEDRUS What were these?

SOCRATES First, there is perceiving together and bringing into one form items which are scattered in many places,[173] in order that one may define each thing and make clear whatever it is
d5 that one wishes to instruct[174] one's audience about on any given occasion. Just so with the things we said just now about what love amounts to when defined: whether what was said was right or wrong, because of it the speech[175] was able to say what was at any rate clear and self-consistent.

PHAEDRUS And what's the second kind of thing you're talking about, Socrates?

SOCRATES Being able to cut up whatever it is again, kind by kind,[176] according to its natural joints, and not to try to break any part into pieces, like an inexpert butcher; as just now the two speeches took the unreasoning aspect of the mind as one
266a form together, and in the way that a single body naturally has its parts in pairs, with both members of each pair having the same name, and labelled respectively left and right, so too the speeches regarded derangement as naturally a single form in us, and the one cut off the part on the left-hand side, then cutting
a5 it again and not giving up until it had found among the parts a love that is, as we say, 'left-handed', and abused it with full justice, while the other speech led us to the parts of madness

on the right-hand side, and discovering and setting forth a love that shares the same name as the other but is divine, it praised b1 it as the cause of our greatest goods.

PHAEDRUS Very true.

SOCRATES Now I am myself, Phaedrus, a lover of these divisions and collections, so that I may be able both to speak and b5 to think; and if I find anyone else who I think has the natural capacity to look to one and to many,[177] I pursue him 'in his footsteps, behind him, as if he were a god'.[178] And the name I give those who can do this – whether it's the right one or not, god knows,[179] but at any rate up till now I have called them c1 'experts in dialectic'.[180] But now tell me what we should have to call them if we learned from you and Lysias; or is this that very thing, the science of speaking, by means of which Thrasymachus and the rest have become clever at speaking themselves, and make others the same, if they are willing to c5 bring them gifts as if they were kings?

PHAEDRUS Royal these people are,[181] but they certainly don't possess knowledge of the things you're asking about. You do seem, though, to be calling this kind of thing by the right name when you call it dialectical; the rhetorical kind seems to me still to be eluding us.[182]

SOCRATES What do you mean? Could there perhaps be something fine that's divorced from the principles in question and is d1 nonetheless grasped in a scientific way? We must certainly not treat it without proper respect, you and I, and we must say just what that part of rhetoric is which is being left out.

PHAEDRUS There are a great many things left, I think, Socrates: d5 the things in the books that have been written on the science of speaking.

SOCRATES A timely reminder. First of all, I think, there's the point that a 'preamble' must be given at the beginning of a speech; these are the things you mean, aren't they – the refinements of the science?

PHAEDRUS Yes. e1

SOCRATES In second place, there is to be something called an 'exposition', with 'testimonies' hard on its heels; thirdly 'proofs', fourthly 'probabilities'; and I think 'confirmation' and

'further confirmation' are mentioned, at least by that excellent
e5 Byzantine artist in speeches.

PHAEDRUS You mean the worthy Theodorus?[183]

267a SOCRATES Of course; and he tells us we must put in a 'refutation' and 'further refutation' both when prosecuting and
when defending. And must we not give public recognition to
that most admirable Parian, Evenus, for being the first to discover 'covert allusion' and 'indirect praise'? Some say he also
a5 utters 'indirect censures' in verse as an aid to memory; he's a
clever one. And shall we leave Tisias and Gorgias to their sleep,
when they saw that probabilities were to be given precedence
over truths, and when they make small things appear large and
b1 large things small by force[184] of speech, and put new things in
an old way and things of the opposite sort in a new way, and
discovered conciseness of speech and infinite length on every
subject? Though when once Prodicus heard me talking like this,
he laughed and said that he alone had discovered what kind of
speeches are needed: what are needed, he said, are neither long
b5 speeches nor short ones but ones of a fitting length.

PHAEDRUS Masterly, Prodicus!

SOCRATES And must we not mention Hippias? I think our
friend from Elis would cast his vote with Prodicus.

PHAEDRUS Certainly.

b10 SOCRATES And how then are we to tell of the terms Polus
c1 has enshrined – terms like 'speaking with reduplication' and
'speaking with maxims' and 'speaking with images' – and the
names that Licymnius gave him as a present for the production
of fine diction?

c5 PHAEDRUS And weren't there some such things that belonged
to Protagoras?

SOCRATES Yes, my boy, there was a 'correctness of diction',
and many other fine things. Then again, the scientific mastery
of wailing speeches dragged out in connection with old age and
poverty seems to me to belong to the might of the Chalcedonian,[185] and the man has also become clever at rousing anger in
d1 large numbers of people all at once, and again, when once they
are angry, at charming them with incantations, as he put it; and
at both devising and refuting calumnies, from whatever source,

he is unbeatable. As for the ending of speeches, everyone seems to be in complete agreement; some call it 'recapitulation', while others call it by other names.

PHAEDRUS You mean summarizing the points at the end, and so reminding the audience of what has been said? d5

SOCRATES That's what I mean – and anything else you can add on the subject of speaking scientifically.

PHAEDRUS Only small things, and not worth mentioning.

SOCRATES Then let's leave the small points; let's hold what we have more closely up to the light, and see just what the power of the science is that's contained in them. 268a

PHAEDRUS A very forceful power it is, Socrates, when it's a question of mass gatherings.

SOCRATES You're right. But see, my fine friend, whether after all you don't think, as I do, that their warp has some gaps in it. a5

PHAEDRUS Do show me.

SOCRATES Tell me then: if someone came up to your friend Eryximachus or his father, Acumenus,[186] and said, 'I know how to apply certain things to people's bodies so as to make them warm, if I want to, and to cool them down and, if I see fit, to make them vomit, or again make their bowels move, and all sorts of things like that; and because I know all that, I claim to be an expert doctor and to be able to make an expert of anyone else to whom I impart knowledge of these things' – when they heard him say that, what do you think *they* would say? a10 b1 b5

PHAEDRUS What else but to ask him whether he also knew both to whom he ought to do all these things and when, and to what extent?

SOCRATES So if he said 'No, not at all; but I expect someone to be able to do the things you ask about by himself, if he has learned the things I teach'? c1

PHAEDRUS I think they'd say the man is mad, and thinks he's become a doctor from having heard something somewhere from a book, or from having stumbled across some common-or-garden remedies, when he has no knowledge of the science itself.

SOCRATES And what about if someone came up to Sophocles or Euripides and said that he knew how to compose very long c5 passages about a small subject and very short ones about a large one, and piteous speeches, when he wished, or again

d1 frightening and threatening ones, and everything else like that, and that he thought that by teaching these things he was passing on the making of tragedy?

PHAEDRUS They too, I think, Socrates, would laugh if anyone thought that tragedy was anything other than the arrangement

d5 of these things – their being put together so as to fit both each other and the whole.

SOCRATES But I don't think they'd abuse him coarsely; just as a musical expert, if he met someone who thought he knew all about harmony just because he happened to know how to

e1 produce the highest and the lowest notes with strings, would not say savagely 'You're off your head, you wretch,' but, being a musician, more gently, 'My dear fellow, the person who means to be an expert in harmony must certainly know that

e5 too, but there is nothing to prevent someone in your condition from having not the slightest understanding of harmony; for what you know is what has to be learned before harmony itself, not the elements of harmony as such.'

PHAEDRUS Quite right.

269a SOCRATES So Sophocles too would say that the man displaying himself to him and Euripides knew the preliminaries to tragedy and not its elements, and Acumenus that the individual in his case knew the preliminaries to medicine but not the elements of medicine.

PHAEDRUS Absolutely.

a5 SOCRATES And what do we think, if the 'honey-toned Adrastus', or Pericles,[187] heard of some of those really fine techniques we were going through just now – things like 'speaking with brevity' and 'speaking with images', and all the other things we went through and said we should look at under the

b1 light – do we think that they, like you and me, would coarsely utter some uneducated expression at those who have written these things up and teach them as a science of rhetoric, or, because they are wiser than us, do we think they would

b5 reproach us and say, 'Phaedrus and Socrates, one should not get angry but be forgiving, if some people who do not know

how to converse[188] prove unable to give a definition of what
rhetoric is, and as a result of being in this state think that they
have discovered rhetoric when they have merely learned the
necessary preliminaries to the science, believing that when they   c1
teach these things to other people they have given them a
complete course in rhetoric; and that the matter of putting all
of these things persuasively, and of arranging the whole, as
something involving no difficulty, their pupils must supply in
their speeches from their own resources'?   c5

PHAEDRUS I rather think, Socrates, that the substance of the
science that these men teach and write up as rhetoric is something like that, and to me, at any rate, you seem to be right; but
how and from where can one provide for oneself the science   d1
belonging to the real expert in rhetoric and the really persuasive
speaker?

SOCRATES As for the ability to acquire it, Phaedrus, so as
to become a complete performer, probably – perhaps even
necessarily – the matter is as it is in all other cases: if it is
naturally in you to be a good orator, a notable orator you will
be when you have acquired knowledge and practice besides,   d5
and whichever you lack of these, you will be incomplete in this
respect. But as for the part of it that is a science, the way of
proceeding seems to me not to be the one that Lysias and
Thrasymachus choose.

PHAEDRUS Then how should one proceed?

SOCRATES I suppose it's no surprise, my good fellow, that   e1
Pericles turned out to be the most complete of all with respect
to rhetoric.

PHAEDRUS Why do you say that?

SOCRATES All sciences of importance require the addition of   270a
babbling and lofty talk[189] about nature; for the relevant high-
mindedness and effectiveness in all directions seem to come
from some such source as that. This is something that Pericles
acquired in addition to his natural ability; for I think because
he fell in with Anaxagoras, who was just such a person, so
becoming filled with lofty talk, and arriving at the nature of   a5
mind and the absence of mind, which were the very subjects
about which Anaxagoras[190] used to talk so much, he was able

to draw from there and apply to the science of speaking what
was applicable to it.

PHAEDRUS What do you mean by that?

b1 SOCRATES The method of the science of medicine is, I suppose,
the same as that of the science of rhetoric.

PHAEDRUS How is that?

SOCRATES In both sciences it is necessary to determine the
b5 nature of something, in the one science the nature of body, in
the other the nature of soul, if you are to proceed scientifically,
and not merely by knack and experience,[191] to produce health
and strength in the one by applying medicines and diet to it, and
to pass on to the other whatever conviction you wish, along with
excellence, by applying words[192] and practices in conformance
with law and custom.

b10 PHAEDRUS Probably it is like that, Socrates.

c1 SOCRATES Do you think, then, that it's possible to understand
the nature of soul satisfactorily without understanding the
nature of the whole?[193]

PHAEDRUS If one is to place any reliance on Hippocrates
the Asclepiad,[194] one can't understand about the body either
c5 without proceeding in this way.

SOCRATES And he's right, my friend; but besides Hippocrates
we should examine the argument[195] to see if it agrees with him.

PHAEDRUS I accept that.

SOCRATES Well then, on the subject of nature, see what
c10 Hippocrates and the true argument say about it. Shouldn't one
d1 reflect about the nature of anything like this: First, is the thing
about which we shall want to be experts ourselves and be
capable of making others expert about something that is simple
or complex? Next, if it is simple, we should consider, shouldn't
d5 we, what natural capacity it has for acting, and on what, or
what capacity it has for being acted upon, and by what; and if
it has more forms[196] than one, we should count these, and see
in the case of each, as in the case where it had only one, with
which of them it is its nature to do what, or with which to have
what done to it by what?

PHAEDRUS Probably, Socrates.

SOCRATES At any rate, proceeding without doing these things

would seem to be just like a blind man's progress. But on no   e1
account must we represent the man who pursues anything
scientifically as like someone blind, or deaf; it's clear that if
anyone teaches anyone speech-making in a scientific way, he
will reveal precisely the essential nature of that thing to which
his pupil will apply his speeches; and that, I think, will be soul.   e5

PHAEDRUS Of course.

SOCRATES Then all his effort is concentrated on that; for it is   271a
in that that he tries to produce conviction. True?

PHAEDRUS Yes.

SOCRATES In that case, it is clear that both Thrasymachus and
anyone else who seriously teaches a science of rhetoric will first   a5
write with complete accuracy and enable us to see whether soul
is something that is one and uniform in nature or complex like
the form of the body; for this is what we say is to reveal the
nature of something.

PHAEDRUS Yes, absolutely.

SOCRATES And in the second place, he will show with which   a10
of its forms it is its nature to do what, or to have what done to
it by what.

PHAEDRUS Of course.

SOCRATES And then, thirdly, having classified the kinds[197] of   b1
speeches and of soul, and the ways in which these are affected,
he will go through all the causes, fitting each to each and
explaining what sort of soul's being subjected to what sorts of
speeches necessarily results in one being convinced and another
not, giving the cause in each case.   b5

PHAEDRUS It would certainly seem to be best like that.

SOCRATES Indeed, my friend, if a model speech[198] or a real one
is ever spoken or written in any way other than this, it will
never be given or written scientifically – not on any other   c1
subject, and not on this one.[199] But those who now write speech
manuals, the people you have listened to, are cunning, and keep
the secret to themselves, although they know perfectly well
about soul; so until they both speak and write in the following
way, let's not believe their claim that they write scientifically.

PHAEDRUS What way is this?   c5

SOCRATES To give the actual words would not be easy; but I'm

willing to say how one should write[200] if it's to be as scientific
as it is possible to be.

PHAEDRUS Say it then.

cio SOCRATES 'Since the power of speech is in fact a leading of the
di   soul, the man who means to be an expert in rhetoric must know
how many forms soul has. Thus their number is so and so, and
they are of such and such kinds, which is why some people are
like this, and others like that; and these having been distinguished in this way, then again there are so many forms of
d5   speeches, each one of such and such a kind. People of one kind
are easily persuaded for one sort of reason by one kind of
speech to hold one kind of opinion, while people of another
kind are for some other sorts of reasons difficult to persuade.

'Having then grasped these things satisfactorily, after that
ei   the student must observe them as they are in real life, and
actually being put into practice, and be able to follow them
with keen perception, or otherwise be as yet no further on from
the things he heard earlier when he was with me. But when he
both has sufficient ability to say what sort of man is persuaded
by what sorts of things, and is capable of telling himself when
272a he observes him that *this* is the man, *this* the nature of person
that was discussed before, now actually present in front of him,
to whom he must now apply *these* kinds of speech in *this* way
in order to persuade him of *this* kind of thing; when he now
has all of this, and has also grasped the occasions for speaking
a5   and for holding back, and again for speaking concisely and
piteously and in an exaggerated fashion, and for all the forms
of speeches he may learn, recognizing the right and the wrong
time for these, *then* his grasp of the science will be well and
completely finished, but not before that; but in whichever of
bi   these things someone is lacking when he speaks or teaches or
writes, and says that he speaks scientifically, the person who
disbelieves him is in the stronger position.' 'Well then, Phaedrus
and Socrates,' perhaps our writer will say, 'do you agree, or
should we accept it if the science of speaking is stated in some
other way?'

b5   PHAEDRUS It's impossible, I think, Socrates, to accept any other
description; yet it seems no light undertaking.

SOCRATES You're right. It's just for this reason that we must turn all our arguments upside down in order to see whether some easier and shorter route to the science doesn't show up somewhere, so that a person doesn't waste his time going off on a long and rough road when he could take a short and smooth one. But if you have any help to give from what you have heard from Lysias or anyone else, try to remember it and tell me.

PHAEDRUS If it depended on trying, I would; but as things are, I'm just not in a position to help.

SOCRATES Then would you like me to mention something I've heard from some of those who make these things their business?

PHAEDRUS Of course.

SOCRATES The saying goes, Phaedrus, that it's right to give the wolf's side of the case as well.

PHAEDRUS Then you do just that.

SOCRATES Well then, they say that there is no need to treat these things so portentously, or carry them back to general principles, going the long way round; for it's just what we said at the very beginning of this discussion – that the person who means to be competent at rhetoric need have nothing to do with the truth about just or good things, or indeed about people who are such by nature or upbringing. For, they say, in the law-courts no one cares in the slightest for the truth about these things but only for what is convincing; and what is convincing is what is *probable*, which is what the person who means to speak scientifically must pay attention to. They go on to say that in fact sometimes one should not even say what was actually done, if it is improbable, but rather what is probable, both when accusing and when defending; whatever one's purpose when speaking, the *probable* is what must be pursued, and that means frequently saying goodbye to the truth. When this happens throughout one's entire speech, it gives one the entire science.

PHAEDRUS You've stated just what those who profess to be experts in speaking say; for I'm reminded, now you say it, that we did touch briefly on this sort of thing before, and it seems a point of crucial significance to those concerned with these things.

SOCRATES But you've gone over the man Tisias himself carefully; so let Tisias tell us this too: doesn't he say that the
b1   probable is just what most people think to be the case?

PHAEDRUS Just that.

SOCRATES I suppose it was on making this clever, and scientific,
discovery that he wrote to the effect that if a weak but brave
b5   man beats up a strong coward and steals his cloak or something
else of his, and is taken to court for it, then neither party should
speak the truth; the coward should say that he wasn't beaten
up by the brave man single-handed, while the other man should
establish that they were on their own together, and should
c1   resort to the well-known argument, 'How could a man like me
have assaulted a man like him?' The coward will certainly not
admit his cowardice but will try to invent some other lie and
so perhaps offer an opening for his opponent to refute him.
And in all other cases too the way to speak 'scientifically' will
c5   be something like this. True, Phaedrus?

PHAEDRUS Of course.

SOCRATES Hey! How cleverly hidden a science Tisias seems to
have discovered – or whoever else it really was, and wherever
he pleases to borrow his name from.[201] Still, my friend, should
c10 we or should we not say to him –

d1   PHAEDRUS What?

SOCRATES This: 'Tisias, we have for some time been saying,
before you came along, that this "probability" comes about in
the minds of ordinary people because of a likeness to the truth;
d5   and we showed only a few moments ago that in every case it is
the man who knows the truth who knows best how to discover
these likenesses. So if you have anything else to say on the
subject of a science of speaking, we'll gladly hear it; if not, we'll
believe what we showed just now, that unless someone counts
e1   up the various natures of those who are going to listen to him,
and is capable both of dividing things[202] up according to their
forms and of including each thing, one by one, under one kind,
he will never be an expert in the science of speaking to the
degree possible for humankind. This ability he will never
e5   acquire without a great deal of application – a labour that the
sensible person ought to undertake not for the purpose of

speaking and acting in relation to human beings but in order
to be able both to say what is gratifying[203] to the gods, and to
act in everything, so far as he can, in a way that is gratifying to
them. For you see, Tisias – so say wiser people than us – no one
in his right mind should practise at gratifying his fellow-slaves,   274a
except as a secondary consideration, but rather at gratifying
good masters, of noble stock.[204] So if the way round is a long
one, don't be surprised; for the journey is to be made for the
sake of important things, not for the things you have in mind.
Yet those too, as our argument asserts, if that is what one   a5
wants, will come about best as an outcome of the others.'[205]

PHAEDRUS I think that what you say is very fine, Socrates, if
only one had the capacity for it.

SOCRATES But surely if one merely tries for the beautiful,[206] to
put up with what it takes is beautiful too.   b1

PHAEDRUS Indeed.

SOCRATES So let that be enough on the subject of the scientific
and unscientific aspects of speaking.

PHAEDRUS By all means.   b5

SOCRATES What we have left is the subject of propriety and
impropriety in writing:[207] in what way, when it is done, it will
be done well, and in what way improperly. True?

PHAEDRUS Yes.

SOCRATES So do you know how you will most gratify god in
relation to speaking, whether actually doing it or talking about   b10
it?

PHAEDRUS Not at all; do you?

SOCRATES At least I can tell you something I've heard, from   c1
people before me; only they know the truth of it. But if we were
to find this out for ourselves, would we care any longer at all
about mere human conjectures?[208]

PHAEDRUS What an absurd question! Tell me what you say
you have heard.

SOCRATES Well, what I heard was that one of the ancient gods   c5
of Egypt was at Naucratis in that country, the god to whom
the sacred bird they call the ibis belongs; the divinity's own
name was Theuth. The story was that he was the first to discover
number and calculation, and geometry and astronomy, as well   d1

as the games of draughts and dice and, to cap it all, letters. King of all Egypt at that time was Thamus – of all of it, that is, that surrounds the great city of the upper region, which the

d5 Greeks call Egyptian Thebes; Thamus they call Ammon. Theuth came to him and displayed his technical inventions, saying that they should be passed on to the rest of the Egyptians; and Thamus asked what benefit each brought. As Theuth went

e1 through them, Thamus criticized or praised whatever he seemed to be getting right or wrong. It is reported that Thamus expressed many views to Theuth about each science, both for and against; it would take a long time to go through them in detail, but when it came to the subject of letters, Theuth said,

e5 'But *this* study, King Thamus, will make the Egyptians wiser and improve their memory; what I have discovered is an elixir[209] of memory and wisdom.' Thamus replied, 'Most scientific Theuth, one man has the ability to beget the elements of a science, but it belongs to a different person to be able to judge what measure of harm and help it contains for those who are

275a going to make use of it; so now you, as the father of letters, have been led by your affection for them to describe them as having the opposite of their real effect. For your invention will produce forgetfulness in the souls of those who have learned it, through lack of practice at using their memory, as through reliance on writing they are reminded from outside by alien

a5 marks, not from within, themselves by themselves.[210] So you have discovered an elixir not of memory but of reminding. To your students you give an appearance of wisdom, not the reality of it; thanks to you, they will hear many things without being

b1 taught them, and will appear to know much when for the most part they know nothing, and they will be difficult to get along with because they have acquired the appearance of wisdom instead of wisdom itself.'

PHAEDRUS Socrates, how easily you make up stories, from Egypt or from anywhere else you like!

b5 SOCRATES Well, my friend, those in the sanctuary of Zeus of Dodona claimed that words from an *oak* were the first prophetic utterances. So the men of those days, because they were not wise like you moderns, were content because of their sim-

plicity to listen to oak and rock,[211] provided only that they said   c1
what was true; but for you, Phaedrus, perhaps it makes a
difference who the speaker is and where he comes from: you
don't just consider whether things are as he says or not.

PHAEDRUS You're right to rebuke me, and it seems to me to
be as your Theban says about letters.

SOCRATES So the man who thinks that he has left behind him   c5
a science in writing, and no less the man who receives it from
him, in the belief that anything clear or certain will come from
what is written down, would be full of simplicity and would be
really ignorant of Ammon's prophetic utterance – thinking that
written words were anything more than a reminder to the man   d1
who knows the subjects to which the things written relate.

PHAEDRUS Quite right.

SOCRATES Yes, Phaedrus, because I think writing has this
strange feature, which makes it truly like painting. The off-   d5
spring of painting stand there as if alive, but if you ask them
something, they preserve a quite solemn silence. Similarly with
written words: you might think that they spoke as if they had
some thought in their heads, but if you ever ask them about
any of the things they say out of a desire to learn, they point to
just one thing, the same each time. And when once it is written,   e1
every composition trundles about everywhere in the same way,
in the presence both of those who know about the subject and
of those who have nothing at all to do with it, and it does not
know how to address those it should address and not those it
should not. When it is ill treated and unjustly abused, it always
needs its father to help it; for it is incapable of either defending   e5
or helping itself.

PHAEDRUS You're quite right about that too.

SOCRATES Now then, do we see another kind of speech,[212] a   276a
legitimate brother of this last one? Do we see both how it comes
into being and how much better and more capable it is from its
birth?

PHAEDRUS What kind are you referring to, and how does it
'come into being'?

SOCRATES The kind of speech that is written together with   a5
knowledge in the soul of the learner, capable of defending itself,

and knowing how to speak and keep silent in relation to the people it should.

PHAEDRUS You mean the living, animate[213] speech of the man who knows, of which written speech would rightly be called a kind of phantom.

b1 SOCRATES Absolutely. So tell me this: the sensible farmer who had some seeds he cared about and wanted to bear fruit – would he sow them with serious purpose during the summer in some garden of Adonis,[214] and delight in watching the garden become

b5 beautiful in eight days, or would he do that for the sake of amusement on a feast-day, if he did it at all; whereas for the purposes about which he was in earnest, would he make use of the science of farming and sow them in appropriate soil, being content if what he sowed reached maturity in the eighth month?

c1 PHAEDRUS Just so, I think, Socrates: he would do the one sort of thing in earnest, the other in the other way, the way you say.

SOCRATES And are we to say that the man who has pieces of knowledge[215] about what is just, beautiful[216] and good has a

c5 less sensible attitude towards his seeds than the farmer?

PHAEDRUS Hardly!

SOCRATES In that case he will not be in earnest about writing them in water – black water, sowing them through a pen with words that are incapable of speaking in their own support, and incapable of adequately teaching what is true.

c10 PHAEDRUS It certainly isn't likely.

d1 SOCRATES No, it isn't; but his gardens of letters, it seems, he will sow and write for amusement, when he does write, laying up a store of reminders both for himself, for when he 'reaches a forgetful old age',[217] and for anyone following the same track,

d5 and he will be pleased as he watches their tender growth; and when others resort to other sorts of amusements, watering themselves with drinking-parties and the other things that go along with these, then he, it seems, will spend his time amusing himself with the things I say, instead of those others.

e1 PHAEDRUS It's a quite beautiful form of amusement you're talking of, Socrates, in contrast with a worthless one: if someone is able to amuse himself with words, telling stories about justice and the other subjects you speak of.[218]

SOCRATES Yes, Phaedrus, just so. But I think it is far finer if one es
is in earnest about those subjects: when one makes use of the
science of dialectic and, taking a fitting soul, plants and sows in
it words accompanied by knowledge, which are sufficient to help
themselves and the one who planted them, and are not without 277a
fruit but contain a seed from which others grow in other soils,
capable of rendering that seed for ever immortal, and making the
one who has it as happy as it is possible for a man to be.

PHAEDRUS This is indeed much finer still. a5

SOCRATES So now, Phaedrus, since we've agreed about these
issues, we can decide those others.

PHAEDRUS Which ones?

SOCRATES The ones we wanted to look into, and so got ourselves
to the present point: how we were to weigh up the reproach aimed a10
at Lysias about his writing of speeches, and about speeches them- b1
selves, which were written scientifically and which not. Well
then, what is scientific and what is unscientific seems to me to
have been demonstrated in fair measure.

PHAEDRUS I thought so; but remind me again how.

SOCRATES Until a person knows the truth about each of the b5
things about which he speaks or writes, and becomes capable
of defining the whole by itself, and, having defined it, knows
how to cut it up again according to its forms until it can no
longer be cut; and until he has reached an understanding of the
nature of soul along the same lines, discovering the form of c1
speech that fits each nature, and so arranges and orders what
he says, offering a complex[219] soul complex speeches containing
all the modes, and simple speeches to a simple soul: not until
then will he be capable of pursuing the making of speeches as
a whole in a scientific way, to the degree that its nature allows, c5
whether for the purposes of teaching or for those of persuading
either, as the whole of our previous argument has indicated.

PHAEDRUS Absolutely; that was just about how it appeared
to us.

SOCRATES And what about the matter of its being fine or d1
shameful to give speeches and write them, and the circumstances under which it would rightly be called a disgrace or
not? Hasn't what we said a little earlier shown –

d5 PHAEDRUS Shown what?

SOCRATES That whether Lysias or anyone else ever wrote or
writes in the future, either for private purposes or publicly, in
the course of proposing laws, so writing a political composition,
and thinks there is any great certainty or clarity in it, then it is
d10 a reproach to its writer, whether anyone says so or not; for to
e1 be ignorant, whether awake or asleep, about the nature of just
and unjust and bad and good cannot truly escape being a matter
of reproach, even if the whole mob applauds it.

PHAEDRUS No indeed.

e5 SOCRATES But the person who thinks that there is necessarily
much that is merely for amusement in a written speech on any
subject, and that none has ever yet been written, whether in
verse or in prose, which is worth much serious attention, or
indeed spoken, in the way that rhapsodes[220] speak theirs, to
produce conviction without questioning or teaching, but that
278a the best of them have really been a way of reminding people
who know; who thinks that clearness and completeness and
seriousness exist only in those things that are taught about what
is just and beautiful and good, and are said for the purpose of
a5 someone's learning from them, and genuinely written in the
soul; who thinks that discourses[221] of that kind should be said
to be as it were his legitimate sons, first of all the one within
b1 him, if it is found there, and in second place any offspring and
brothers of this one that have sprung up simultaneously, in the
way they should, in other souls, other men; and who says goodbye to the other kind – *this*, surely, Phaedrus, will be the sort of
person you and I would pray that we both might come to be.

b5 PHAEDRUS Yes, absolutely. I wish and pray for what you say.

SOCRATES So now let that count as our due amusement from
the subject of speaking. And as for you, Phaedrus, you go and
tell Lysias that we two came down to the spring and the sacred
c1 place of the Nymphs and heard arguments[222] that instructed us
to tell this to Lysias and anyone else who composes speeches,
and to Homer and anyone else who has composed verses,
whether without music or to be sung, and, thirdly, to Solon and
whoever writes compositions in the form of political speeches,
c5 which he calls laws: if he has composed these things knowing

how the truth is, able to help his composition when he is challenged on its subjects, and with the capacity, speaking in his own person, to show that what he has written is of little worth,[223] then such a man ought not to derive his title from these, and be called after them, but rather from those things in which he is seriously engaged.

PHAEDRUS What are the titles you assign him, then?

SOCRATES To call him wise seems to me to be too much, and to be fitting only in the case of a god; to call him either a philosopher[224] or something like that would both fit him more and be in better taste.

PHAEDRUS And not at all inappropriate.

SOCRATES On the other hand, the man who doesn't possess things of more value than the things he composed or wrote, turning them upside down over a long period of time, sticking them together and taking them apart – him, I think, you'll rightly call a poet or author of speeches or writer of laws?

PHAEDRUS Of course.

SOCRATES Then tell that to your friend.

PHAEDRUS And what of you? What will you do? For we certainly shouldn't pass over your friend, either.

SOCRATES Who do you mean?

PHAEDRUS The beautiful Isocrates.[225] What will you report to *him*, Socrates? What title shall we give him?

SOCRATES Isocrates is still young, Phaedrus; but I'm willing to say what I prophesy for him.

PHAEDRUS What's that?

SOCRATES He seems to me to be on a level superior to Lysias and his speeches in terms of his natural endowment, and to have a greater nobility in the blend of his character; so there would be no surprise, as he grows older, if the very speeches he works at now turned out to make those of any other speech-writer worse than puerile by comparison. Still more so, were he to be dissatisfied with what he does now, and some diviner impulse led him to more important things; for there is a certain innate philosophical instinct in the man's mind. So that is the report I take from the gods here to Isocrates as my beloved, and you take the other to Lysias as yours.

b5 PHAEDRUS I'll do it. But let's go, now that the heat has become milder.

SOCRATES Shouldn't we pray to the gods here before we go?

PHAEDRUS Of course.

SOCRATES Dear Pan and all you gods of this place, grant me that I may become beautiful within; and that what is in my
c1 possession outside me may be in friendly accord with what is inside. And may I count the wise man as rich; and may my pile of gold be of a size that no one but a man of moderate desires[226] could bear or carry it.

c5   Do we still need anything else, Phaedrus? For me that prayer is enough.

PHAEDRUS Make it a prayer for me too; for what friends have they share.

SOCRATES Let's go.

Appendix:
The Structure of the *Phaedrus*

The translation in this volume offers the reader no resting-points in the form of chapters or any other form of subdivision; Plato did not divide his text in this way, and, after all, by modern standards, the *Phaedrus* is not very long – maybe the size of a novella (though infinitely more complex than any novella known to me). Still, the following rough sketch of the structure of the dialogue may be found useful:

227a–230e: Socrates meets Phaedrus; preliminary conversation.
230e–234c: Phaedrus reads Lysias' speech.
234c–237b: Transition to Socrates' first speech.
237b–241d: Socrates' first speech on *erôs*.
241d–243e: Transition to Socrates' second speech.
243e–245c: Socrates' second speech begins.
245c–249d: 'Experiences and actions' of divine and human souls.
249d–257a: The blessings of the madness of *erôs*.
257a–b: A prayer to Love.
257b–259d: Transition to a discussion of speaking and writing.
259e–274b: Rhetoric – as it should be, and as it is.
274b–277a: How useful is the written text (or the set speech) as a medium of communication and teaching?
277a–279b: Conclusions.
279b–c: A final prayer, after which Socrates and Phaedrus leave.

Notes

1. *Cephalus*: Cephalus plays a prominent role in the *Republic*, the main action of which takes place at his house.

2. *outside the wall*: The *Lysis* too is set outside the walls of Athens but right beneath them; Socrates evidently only left the city when he had to (on military service: see e.g. Alcibiades' speech at the end of the *Symposium*), and – as we shall soon be told – is a stranger even in the countryside of Attica.

3. *Acumenus*: Father (if the same person is meant as at 268a) of another medical doctor, Eryximachus, one of the party-goers and speakers in the *Symposium* (Phaedrus is his friend and near contemporary).

4. *Epicrates' house*: Evidently Epicrates (see Nails 2003) was himself, like Lysias, an orator, who shared Lysias' democratic leanings; Morychus, whose house he owned, has a name in comedy for his extravagance. (So evidently Lysias mixes with the very wealthy.)

5. *temple of Olympian Zeus*: Still one of the landmarks of Athens, near Syntagma Square.

6. *Obviously . . . speeches*: 'Obviously', because of Lysias' fame as an orator/speech-writer. 'Speeches', or more generally *types of discourse*, will be one of the key subjects of the *Phaedrus*.

7. *to quote Pindar*: Pindar, *Isthmians* 1.2 (adapted, as quotations often are in Plato).

8. *love*: 'Love' here is *erôs*, which will be another key subject of the dialogue – that is, passionate love, of which consensual sex would be a normal and expected (or hoped-for) component – at least as normally understood. Phaedrus' remark here (that Lysias' speech will be an 'appropriate' one for Socrates to hear) reflects what is – at any rate in the world of the Platonic dialogues – a familiar feature of Socrates' character, namely his eroticism, in

particular his attraction to beautiful boys. And yet, later in the *Phaedrus*, as in the *Symposium* and the *Lysis*, he will be found advocating a kind of erotic relationship that in its ideal form actually *excludes* sexual intercourse as a diversion from the real object, and goal, of *erôs*: knowledge.

9. *favours*: I.e., as will become patently obvious, sexual favours. Throughout the dialogue, sexual activity will be referred to only indirectly, in Lysias' case as a kind of show of good taste; Socrates will then follow suit in his first speech. Paradoxically, the closest the *Phaedrus* comes to the overt use of sexual language will be when Socrates, in his second speech, describes the true lover's passion as he remembers Beauty Itself, and his soul sprouts its wings (so taking it *away* from the physical aspects of existence). See Introduction, p. xxii.

10. *the general good*: As so often in Plato, there is a point behind the joke: Socrates will ultimately suggest that all truly scientific rhetoric will be 'for the general good'.

11. *as Herodicus recommends*: Is this a reference to training for *sprinting*? The run to Megara would be more like a Marathon, but then Socrates/Plato evidently did not think much of Herodicus (see *Republic* 406a–b).

12. *I'll swear by the Dog*: A favourite, characteristic oath of Socrates'.

13. *hearing people speak*: Or 'hearing speeches', which is how Phaedrus might understand Socrates here. But the *logoi* Socrates is most interested in, as we shall discover by the end of the *Phaedrus*, are not 'speeches' but talk of a quite different sort. (*Logos*: 'speech', 'discourse', 'word', 'thing said'; also 'account', 'reason'.)

14. *seeing, seeing him*: Probably another poetic reference; in any case Socrates' language half-mimics Phaedrus' supposed 'manic frenzy'. (Madness in various forms will be another central topic of the *Phaedrus*.)

15. *you've foiled me*: Writing contrasted with memory: cf. the story of Theuth and Thamus at *Phaedrus* 274c–275b.

16. *the Ilissus*: No longer, sadly, part of an idyllic landscape, in modern Athens (nor usually even flowing in high summer).

17. *Boreas . . . Oreithuia*: Boreas is the god who is the North Wind; Oreithuia was daughter of Erechtheus, primeval King of Athens.

18. *Agra*: One of the 'demes', or basic administrative districts, of Athens.

19. *for goodness' sake*: What Phaedrus actually says is 'by Zeus!', which in English fails quite to convey his tone.

20. *wise people*: Of which, of course, Socrates is not one; his typical claim is that he knows *nothing*.

21. *Delphic inscription*: The inscription would famously have been found on, or in, the temple of Apollo at Delphi.

22. *Typhon*: A hundred-headed dragon, the last obstacle between Zeus and kingship over the gods (Hesiod, *Theogony* 820ff). Socrates will later give an answer to his present question here (am I like the Typhon, or a simpler creature?) by comparing the human soul to a charioteer and his two horses, one wild, the other of a nobler sort; for the full significance of this question, see Introduction, pp. xxiii–xxv.

23. *conversation*: Logoi again (see n. 13 above).

24. *By Hera ... stopping-place*: The tone and language of the description that follows are those of a poet's ideal landscape. It is open to question how seriously we should take Socrates' enthusiasm; later, certainly, he will raise questions about the nature and location of true beauty.

25. *agnus castus*: *Vitex agnus castus*, a plant of the vervain genus.

26. *Achelous*: 'The river god *par excellence*' (Hamilton 1973).

27. *extraordinary*: Literally 'out of place' (*atopos*); similarly at 229c6 above.

28. *people in the city*: At any rate, the Socrates of the dialogues spends all his time talking to them, and asking questions.

29. *prescription*: The *pharmakon* – a term that can be used of either remedial drugs or toxic ones.

30. *speeches in books*: Just what Socrates really thinks about *logoi* in books we shall discover in the concluding parts of the *Phaedrus*.

31. *Listen, then*: Is the speech authentically Lysianic or not? Despite divisions in scholarly opinion, it is in the end hard to believe that this *Erotic Essay* (we have an example by the most outstanding of all Attic orators, Demosthenes) is not a Platonic parody of the genre. Such speeches would typically have been displays of virtuosity by professional writers, and typically, like the present example, they would have been on paradoxical themes. (If the speaker is really not in the grip of erotic passion, why should he want sex with the boy in the first place?)

32. *these things*: I.e. sex.

33. *For it ... own capacity*: I.e. it will all be done in a wholly businesslike way, to fit in with the non-lover's normal schedule and strictly without any damage to his own interests (unlike the other man, driven by the 'compulsion' of love).

34. *please the other party*: And, presumably, the speaker: the term

used for 'to please' is *charizesthai*, which is what the speaker wants the boy to do to him (see 227c7). But since he's trying to persuade the boy, he specifically mentions only the non-lover's attempt to please the *boy* (*autois*, 231c6).

35. *words*: *Logoi* again (n. 13 above).

36. *such a thing*: I.e. sex.

37. *affection*: I.e. *philia*, the term that most closely corresponds to English 'friendship'; *philia* is the most a boy would normally be expected to feel in response to the (normal) erotic attentions of an older man – i.e. *philia* rather than *erôs*. (So the boy would be expected to derive other benefits from the relationship, not sexual pleasure; 'Lysias' will shortly give us a clearer notion of what these benefits might be.)

38. *whatever benefits they receive*: I.e. from 'doing what they did' (pleasure, presumably).

39. *from the thing*: I.e. from 'granting favours' (the Greek has just *ap'autou*, 'from it').

40. *miss*: 'Miss' is *pothein*, which is what the lover feels for the loved one when separated from him; and it may also be worth noticing that the final word of the speech, *erôta* ('ask'), has the same letters as one form (the accusative) of *erôs*, though it would have sounded differently. An appropriately showy ending, perhaps, for an *erôtikos logos*?

41. *inspired*: In Greek *theios*, 'divine'; so '*divinely* inspired'.

42. *its creator*: Its 'maker', or 'poet': *poiêtês*.

43. *I missed it*: I.e. the author's saying what he ought to say on his subject.

44. *clearly I have heard something*: I.e. because it can't have come from *him* – he knows nothing (see below).

45. *Sappho . . . prose-writers*: It is not immediately clear what Socrates could have learned from pre-eminent *love*-poets like Sappho and Anacreon about the *non*-lover; or is it just about what hopeless cases (ordinary) lovers are? Still more mysterious is the reference to prose-writers, for the only one we know of who wrote in praise of the non-lover is Plato himself (*his* version is just about to come). Or is this just the point? Is Plato perhaps, for once, allowing himself a sly self-reference?

46. *Absolutely excellent!*: What Phaedrus actually says is 'Most noble (Socrates)'; I take it that this is just another way of expressing his excitement at the prospect of hearing a new speech.

47. *nine archons*: The *Constitution of the Athenians*, attributed to Aristotle, tells us that the nine archons – key officers of state in

the Athenian system – swore to 'dedicate a golden statue, if they should contravene any of the laws'. Thus Phaedrus is implying the following: 'I'll dedicate statues if I'm wrong, and you do better than Lysias.' However, the significance of what he says (and of Socrates' response: 'You are ... truly made of gold') is immediately increased as soon as we know that the virtuoso fifth–fourth-century practitioner and teacher of rhetoric after whom Plato's *Gorgias* is named – and whom Socrates briefly mentions later in the *Phaedrus* (261b, 267a); he would have been about seventy at the dramatic date of the dialogue, and lived to be well over a hundred – famously dedicated a golden statue of *himself* at Delphi; and that a (much later) report has Plato scoffing at him on his return, as 'the beautiful and *golden* Gorgias'. For these and further aspects of the whole context, see the brilliant account in Morgan 1994.

48. *dedication of the Cypselids at Olympia*: Once again there is a connection with Gorgias, who had a statue at Olympia as well (see preceding note), this time dedicated by his grand-nephew Eumolpus; but *Socrates'* statue will be 'beside the dedication of the Cypselids', which probably refers to a colossal statue of Zeus (whom Socrates will himself later associate with philosophy). Here too I refer to Morgan 1994, which also provides, among other things, a convincing explanation of the detail that Socrates' statue will be 'of hammered metal'. Morgan's article as a whole illustrates just how rich Plato's text can be; we modern readers will no doubt very often miss a great deal of what the text would have offered to an alert contemporary, i.e. fourth-century, reader.

49. *grasp ... words*: The words are attributed to Pindar at Plato, *Meno* 76d.

50. *craftsman*: The word is *poiêtês* again (see n. 42 above).

51. *musical race of the Ligurians*: Apparently a deliberately silly etymology for *ligeiai* ('clear-voiced') as an epithet of the Muses: the only known connection between those Greeks in the western Mediterranean called Ligurians and music is actually what Plato – it seems – is inventing here. Socrates is parodying the invocations of the Muses traditionally made by poets (cf. the opening lines of both the *Iliad* and the *Odyssey*), perhaps thereby indicating something about his attitude towards the performance he is about to give.

52. *take part with me*: Another poeticism, if not a quotation.

53. *his friend*: I.e. Lysias, who was just now Phaedrus' 'darling' (236b5).

54. *what each thing really is*: The starting-point for numerous Platonic dialogues is the question of what something or other (often one or other of the 'virtues') is.

55. *desire*: I.e. *epithumia*, a term often, but not exclusively, used in connection with irrational wants; for Socrates, paradoxically, ideal *erôs* will turn out to be *both* an expression of the highest rationality *and* a kind of irrationality (in fact, madness).

56. *the beautiful*: 'The beautiful' is here plural in Greek, and either (or both) neuter and masculine.

57. *restraint*: I.e. *sôphrosunê*, traditionally and unhelpfully translated as 'temperance'; self-mastery or, more generally, being in one's right mind.

58. *excess*: I.e. *hubris*.

59. *this is called love*: The leaden etymology – *erôs/rhômê* – recalls the earlier one (see n. 51 above), and surely matches the tone of the whole. (No wonder Socrates was keen to claim that he got it from someone else.)

60. *something more than human*: Something *divine*, in fact (*theios* again: cf. n. 41 above).

61. *uttering in dithyrambs*: Dithyrambic poetry, about which – in its classical form – we know relatively little, seems to be associated in Plato particularly with mere artificial invention; he certainly seems to have had little time for it.

62. *Well, my brave friend*: I borrow this translation from Nehamas and Woodruff 1995, who point out the peculiar epic form of address Socrates uses here (*ô pheriste*): '. . . probably signals Socrates' parody of overblown rhetoric'.

63. *it is necessarily*: Throughout this part of his speech, Socrates emphasizes what (he claims) will follow *necessarily* from his definition of *erôs*. His approach is systematic in a way in which – as he has already begun to suggest – Lysias' was not.

64. *he will . . . become wisest*: Once again, in the midst of parody, we find a genuinely Socratic element (cf. n. 54 above). For Socrates, the greatest good, if not the only true good (the only thing *always* good), is wisdom; depriving someone of wisdom will correspondingly be the way of doing them the greatest harm.

65. *what happened before*: Sex.

66. *having . . . sobered up*: 'Having become *sôphrôn*': cf. n. 57 above.

67. *as the sherd flips . . . side*: An ancient source makes this a reference to a game of tag, in which the fall of a sherd (like the flip of a coin) determined who would be 'it'.

68. *necessarily*: I.e. given what *erôs* essentially is.

69. *as . . . boy*: Socrates ends with a flourish, and with what is almost a hexameter (epic) line, and possibly a reference to a proverb.

70. *as I said it would be*: I.e. as inexpert(?).

71. *even though I'm playing the critic*: Epic poetry – or Homer – typically sings the *praise* of men, *kleos andrôn*.

72. *whatever fate . . . without me*: Cf. e.g. 275e3–5, on the fate of compositions left without a father to defend them.

73. *the time*: The words 'the time . . . stands still' may be a gloss, and their meaning is far from certain; the translation given may be the best that can be made of them.

74. *a superhuman capacity*: A *divine* (*theios*) capacity.

75. *Simmias the Theban*: This Simmias is one of Socrates' two interlocutors in the *Phaedo*; see especially *Phaedo* 85c–d.

76. *that supernatural experience, the sign*: For another, and very similar, description of Socrates' famous *daimonion*, see *Apology* 31c–d. Here in the *Phaedrus*, however, there is a clear sense of a *literary* use of the idea; Socrates hardly needs a divine sign to tell him to make amends for the preceding speech, when he was already ashamed even at the prospect of giving it (237a; cf. 243b); it isn't just that his 'soul was troubled' while he was making it, as he is about to say – surely disingenuously (242c6–8).

77. *against . . . gods*: I.e. against the divine (*to theion*).

78. *that . . . men*: In fact (it seems) a Platonic adaptation from Ibycus.

79. *potion*: The Greek is *katapharmakeuthentos*; cf. *pharmakon* at 230d6.

80. *Stesichorus*: Another lyric poet (sixth century).

81. *true follower of the Muses*: Or 'a musical expert' (*mousikos*); but see the story about the cicadas at 259a–d.

82. *This . . . Troy*: This is evidently a fragment of a poem now lost. (As the plot of Euripides' *Helen* has it, the real Helen was in Egypt throughout the war, and it was a phantom Helen who went to Troy.)

83. *Palinode*: Or 'taking-it-back poem' (Nehamas and Woodruff 1995).

84. *free men*: Not that Athenian sailors, especially rowers in the fleet, would not for the most part have been free men in the literal sense (citizens); but not all free men – so the claim is – behave as free men should.

85. *one . . . received*: Because after all, on the Socratic model of *erôs*, what the lover brings to the relationship will be just as important as what the beloved brings; it will be much more of an equal

relationship than that between an ordinary lover and his boy. (The Greek is *ek tôn homoiôn*, which might be more literally rendered as 'on equal terms'.)

86. *Here . . . wish*: I.e. Phaedrus will stand in for him. (There is no suggestion in the *Phaedrus* of anything beyond simple friendship between Socrates and Phaedrus himself.)

87. *Euphemus, of Himera*: 'Euphemus' means something like 'speaking with good omen' (*euphêmein* is actually to say nothing, the best way of keeping out of trouble); while 'Himera' suggests *himeros*, another word for 'desire' or 'longing'.

88. *mantic*: That is, the art of the *mantis*, or seer, with which Socrates suggested he had a passing acquaintance back at 242c–d. Another fanciful etymology, shortly to be followed by another; yet at *some* level Socrates must presumably be serious about the basic claim he is now making, that under the right conditions madness is beneficial rather than harmful.

89. *touched by it*: I.e. by madness.

90. *A third . . . Muses*: This, obviously enough, is poetic inspiration (see Plato's *Ion*, which suggests at best a rather mixed view about its real usefulness); it is rather less clear what exactly is meant to fall under the previous (second) kind of 'madness'.

91. *a first principle*: A reading preferred by many editors, and evidently known to Cicero more than two thousand years ago, would give the easier sense '. . . it would not *be a first principle*'; but our manuscripts give us the text I have translated, and I have preferred to stay with that more difficult, and more interesting, text. (Here is one consideration: the verb *gignesthai*, which is used here, *can* mean 'be'; but since it has just been used twice, and will fairly soon be used again, in the sense of '*come-to*-be', it is not easy to suppose that Plato would have used it to mean 'be' – instead of *einai*, the standard verb for 'be' – just *here*.)

92. *superhuman*: I.e. divine (only a god could do it).

93. *combined*: Literally 'grown together' (*sumphutos*); the point is that it is in the nature of the things combined to be so. (Nehamas and Woodruff 1995 have 'natural union' for the complete phrase *sumphutos dunamis*; this leaves out the *dunamis*, 'force' or 'power', but may still be the better translation.)

94. *driver*: Or our 'ruler', *archôn*, a term that recalls the language Socrates used in describing the relationship between reason and desire in his first speech ('in each of us there are two kinds of thing that rule (*archein*) and lead us', and so on).

95. *god*: I.e. whichever god it may be appropriate to refer to; 'a

very frequent formula for expressing pious reservation' (de Vries 1969).

96. *in a way*: An important qualification, reminding us that the context is one of a *simile*. (Human beings, on Socrates' reckoning, are closer to the divine than birds.)

97. *beautiful . . . kind*: These are not, it should be said, typical attributes of the divine, especially as represented by the poets. Socrates' treatment of the gods is radical in other respects too: he has already denied them bodies, and will shortly associate them – without identifying them – with astronomical entities (planets and/or constellations).

98. *Hestia alone remains*: As goddess of the hearth, where else would she be but at home? (This is, I suggest, one of a number of places where the general tone of apparent seriousness in the speech is relaxed; it is for the reader to judge what the effect of these moments may be on the whole.)

99. *the final labour*: The term *labour* here recalls the Labours of Heracles: the issue, for each soul, will be whether it manages to achieve even the slightest share in the divine feast – which Socrates is about to describe.

100. *that are called immortal*: I.e. the gods; all souls, as we have been told, are immortal, but we call the gods 'the immortals', and they are pure souls.

101. *This . . . relates*: This is the language Platonic dialogues typically reserve for those entities that go under the names of (Platonic) 'Forms' or 'Ideas' (*eidē, ideai*); so when, a few lines below, a divine soul is said to 'see justice itself . . . self-control . . . knowledge', it is presumably 'the Form of Justice', 'the Form of Self-Control' and so on. These, roughly speaking, represent the essence, or what-it-is-to-be, of justice, self-control, etc., conceived of as existing separately from their instantiations – i.e. particular instances of them. Platonic Forms are not normally represented as existing in space, and indeed in the Platonic universe it is not clear that there is any space outside the universe (which is 'the all', *to pan*, everything there is, so that it would be surprising to find that there was anything *beyond* it). But neither, of course, is the soul literally composed of a charioteer and two horses; nor can there be any question of the Forms being 'seen' in anything but a metaphorical sense. The general (and more prosaic) point is that the mind or soul has to grasp Forms – however these are to be understood – in order to reach full, or real, knowledge of anything. Socrates will towards the end of the

dialogue describe the means by which mere human souls may perhaps achieve that end: 'dialectic', or the 'science of (philosophical) conversation', which understands how to 'collect' and 'divide' in order to reach the essence of things (265c ff.).

102. *self-control*: I.e. *sôphrosunê*, previously rendered as 'restraint' (see n. 5 above).

103. *things that we now say are*: I.e. particular instantiations of Forms, like the things around us that we can see, hear, etc. – and that have the habit of *changing* ('to which coming-into-being attaches'), and in which properties will show up in what appear to be widely different ways ('that which seems to be different . . .': what is it, exactly, that is in common between the beauty of this boy, for example, and the beauty of that piece of music?).

104. *nectar . . . ambrosia*: Once again the tone suddenly lightens; high metaphysical seriousness is followed by *play*.

105. *what only appears to nourish them*: Or 'feed on the nourishment of (mere) opinion (*trophê doxastê*)': in Plato, *doxa*, 'opinion', is typically contrasted with knowledge, not least because it can be false as well as true. 'Opinion' is the state of mind of non-philosophers, who fail to look further than (or rise above) ordinary appearances.

106. *best part of the soul*: I.e., clearly, its rational part ('part', however, is imported by the translation; the Greek has just the definite article + superlative adjective, both in the neuter: 'the best (?)' of the soul).

107. *Destiny*: I.e. the way things are, which is fixed and immovable for ever. For a similar idea (and a similar account of *what* is fixed, i.e. an ordering of types of life in terms of worth: see below), see the concluding myth (the story of Er) in the *Republic*; later in the *Phaedrus*, the present discourse will itself be described as a kind of *muthos*, or story (265b–c).

108. *this soul . . . birth*: The idea, originally Pythagorean, that our souls will enter new bodies at some time after our death – human or animal, depending on our behaviour in this life – is one that appears in several Platonic dialogues, not always in a mythical context.

109. *devoted . . . love*: These are not real alternatives: the true lover will turn out to be a philosopher (a lover of wisdom), drawn to true Beauty, and beloved of the Muses.

110. *poet*: The (ordinary) poet, then, even if inspired (the seer, who is certainly inspired, comes only just above), comes strikingly low in the list – even after the gymnastic trainer. But then hardly

any of them will even have heard of the 'region above the heavens' (cf. 247c3–4); so there will be few *philosophical* poets. (Parmenides might be the sole exception.)

111. *For . . . years*: I.e. one's chance of real bliss – which means staying (temporarily) in the company of the gods – comes only once every ten thousand years.

112. *live a life . . . human form*: Probably a reference to the fate e.g. of Heracles, who – according to one version of the story – actually did join the company of the stars after death; Socrates' story manages to pretend to being traditional at the same time as being utterly radical.

113. *allotment and choice*: The same apparently puzzling combination occurs at *Republic* x, 617d ff., where it seems that souls cast lots for the *order* in which they choose among a limited number of lives of each sort (how else would the world order be maintained?).

114. *recollection*: For the Platonic theory of learning as 'recollection' (i.e. of things our souls 'saw' before birth), see *Meno* 80d ff. and *Phaedo* 72e ff.

115. *things we now say are*: I.e., again, the familiar things around us, as opposed to those things that 'really are' (the Forms).

116. *reminders*: I.e. (presumably) his sensations, which give him what he needs to 'collect together into one through reasoning' in order to 'comprehend what is said universally' – the whole being properly described as 'recollection' (b4–c4, just above).

117. *perfection*: There is a verbal play here, on *teleos*, 'perfect', and *teletai*, 'rites' (cf. *neotelês*, 'newly initiated', at 250e1); the point is not so much that philosophers become literally *perfect* – because after all their souls remain human souls – but rather that they are initiated into the highest rites.

118. *regarded as mad*: But of course he *is* also mad; people call him mad for the wrong reasons (that he is truly possessed goes 'unrecognized by the many', d3 above).

119. *beautiful*: 'The beautiful' is a genitive plural in the Greek that could be either masculine or neuter; the masculine would perhaps be more to the point here – except that what the (true) lover really loves, according to Socrates, is actually Beauty, not any particular beautiful person.

120. *ourselves*: The 'we' here is perhaps most naturally taken as referring to Socrates himself and the boy he is addressing: according to what he will say at 252c and e, it is philosophers who follow in Zeus' train, and philosophers will look for boys who are 'naturally disposed towards philosophy' (252e3).

121. *longing for what was before*: So the preceding description was itself a case of recollection; Socrates was himself truly inspired, or maddened, in his description of the 'perfect rites'.

122. *objects of love*: I.e., presumably, 'justice and self-control and the other things which are of value to souls' (b1–2 above).

123. *excess*: This is *hubris* again (238a2, etc.).

124. *himeros*: Yet another fanciful etymology (and no more possible to render in English).

125. *desire*: I.e. the *himeros*.

126. *boy with his beauty*: Or is it that *other* beautiful thing, Beauty Itself, that he remembers? The Greek leaves it open.

127. *desire*: Again, *himeros*.

128. *I think . . . down*: I have taken it that the lines are outrageous (it should be 'excessive': the word is *hubristikon*), *because* they are – or rather the second is – unmetrical (it breaks with the restraints of metre, as it were). But see Introduction.

129. *Ares*: The traditional god of war (cf. n. 112 above).

130. *this practice*: 'This practice' must be that of leading, helping a boy towards philosophy: a reference to Socrates' own position, perhaps, in relation to the boy he is addressing – for after all, Socrates is no expert in anything, and any skills the present speech may suggest come from a source outside him (see especially 257a7–8, where he asks Love not to take away 'the expertise in love you gave me', i.e. for the duration of the speech?).

131. *outcome*: Or its 'ending', *teleutê*: presumably sharing in the same love of wisdom. Socrates carefully avoids presuming that his speech will persuade the boy (but we should also note the contrast with the kind of 'ending' that Lysias had in mind in his speech, i.e. sex: see 264b1–2, where Phaedrus makes a joke of it).

132. *Into three forms*: The Greek here has just 'into three' (*trichêi*), but the addition of 'forms' is justified by what follows, which is, more literally: '(. . . into three:) two horse-shaped (?) kinds of forms/sorts of things (*hippomorphô men duo tine eidê*), and a third, charioteer's, form (*hêniochon de eidos triton*)'.

133. *on the nobler station*: I.e. on the right.

134. *spoken orders*: Or 'orders and reason' (*keleusmati . . . kai logôi*).

135. *excess*: Hubris.

136. *excess*: Hubristês.

137. *a starting-barrier*: I.e. on a racecourse. Falling back from the start might look an unlikely thing for a chariot-horse to do but perhaps not if he is having to be reined in like *this* horse?

138. *gives it over to pains*: As Nehamas and Woodruff 1995 point

out, this is a Homeric phrasing. Now we are, finally, in a kind of epic context (cf. 241e) – though an odd one, with the soul as battlefield.

139. *desire*: *Himeros* – so apparently it was Zeus who coined the word (see 251c).

140. *into its possessor*: Literally 'into the beautiful (one)'.

141. *not as love but as friendship*: I.e. he interprets his extraordinary experience in the conventional terms, of a boy who feels friendship for a lover in return for benefits received (when the immediate cause of everything is actually his own beauty, acting as a reminder of that other Beauty).

142. *three submissions*: The metaphor is from wrestling.

143. *forced . . . Phaedrus*: I.e. he had to play the poet; he's no good as a poet; but it was all Phaedrus' fault anyway? (But later on in the dialogue, Socrates will have much to say about the need to adapt one's speeches to the nature of one's audience; is that, perhaps, the deeper point behind what he says here? See Introduction.)

144. *the expertise . . . that you gave me*: Sc. 'and so enabled me to say what I said'?

145. *Polemarchus*: Polemarchus plays a small role at the beginning of the conversation in the *Republic*.

146. *talk*: 'Talk' is *logoi* in the Greek; clearly, in light of what is to follow (which will be an example of, and will end by discussing, philosophical *exchange*), not in this case just 'speeches'.

147. *you . . . bend*: What the Greek text gives us is 'you don't know [that] the expression "pleasant bend" [comes from the long bend of the Nile]'; the bracketed parts are usually treated as an addition by a copyist trying to explain 'pleasant bend' (or 'sweet elbow'); whatever the origin of the expression, it evidently referred to forms of words that manage to say something other than what the speaker intends – the elbow/bend is precisely not sweet/pleasant. In correspondence, Alan Griffiths has suggested an alternative, and much more attractive, scenario for the origin of the phrase: that *glukus a(n)gkôn* was a rhapsode's garbling of a Homeric phrase – *kateibeto glukus aiôn*: 'his sweet *life* was dripping away' (for 'rhapsodes', see n. 220 below). The description is of Odysseus pining away on Kalypso's beach at *Odyssey* 5.152. The rhapsode (Griffiths suggests), getting to this line, mixed up its ending with that of the next but one, *kai ana(n)gkêi*, either because he misremembered the line or – more likely – because he looked down for a prompt and got the wrong place (*a(n)gkôn* being a garbled combination of *aiôn* and *ana(n)gkêi*). In any case

he ended up saying 'his (the great hero Odysseus') sweet *elbow* was dripping away.' The audience, Griffiths surmises, dissolved into laughter, and ' "sweet elbow" became irresistible shorthand for non-correspondence between intention and utterance . . .' If this is not the right explanation (and we shall never know), it is certainly beautiful (sweet) enough.

148. *author*: Or 'poet' – the word is *poiêtês*; hence the following metaphor of the *theatre*.

149. *a Lycurgus, a Solon or a Darius*: Respectively, lawgivers of Athens and Sparta, and Great King of Persia.

150. *What would . . . justly so*: A somewhat odd set of things for Phaedrus to say, and just here; either something has been added to Plato's text – or, possibly, Phaedrus is doing some philosophical posing (but still, why just here?).

151. *converse with*: The verb is *dialegesthai*, which is what (Platonic) *philosophers* typically do.

152. *speech*: Or 'talk'; but shortly, in e1, *logos* must again be translated as '(a) speech'. (The difficulty for the translator throughout is that *logoi* can be *either* speeches *or* philosophical talk, which will usually not take the form of, and may actually be opposed to, the making of speeches.)

153. *a . . . aside*: Homer, *Iliad* 2.361.

154. *arguments*: *Logoi* yet again.

155. *the Laconian*: I.e. the Spartan; is Socrates saying just 'to put it bluntly'? (The Spartans, supposedly, were characterized by their *laconic* speech.)

156. *beautiful offspring*: Phaedrus is bringing yet more *logoi* into existence (cf. 242a–b), though now of a different kind (arguments).

157. *speech*: *Logoi* (which will not exclude written 'speech').

158. *Palamedes*: An epic hero proverbial for his cleverness.

159. *Gorgias . . . Odysseus*: For Gorgias, see n. 47 above; Thrasymachus of Chalcedon and Theodorus of Byzantium were well-known rhetorical theorists (Thrasymachus is also the aggressive opponent of Socrates in *Republic* 1 who provides the conception of justice that the rest of the *Republic* is in large part designed to refute). Phaedrus' identifications may possibly indicate his different valuations of the three figures: Nestor in Homer is an upright speaker, while Odysseus, at least later, became synonymous with sly cunning.

160. *he will . . . the opposite*: Cf. the formulae at 258a4–5, which can be rendered 'It seemed (good) to the council/people . . .'

161. *so as . . . in motion*: See Plato, *Parmenides* 127d–128a, where the 'Eleatic Palamedes' (Parmenides' clever pupil/follower, Zeno) puts forward just these sorts of theses.

162. *things that are*: 'The things that are' could just mean 'things'; but readers are likely to remember, in such a context, expressions like 'being that really is' from Socrates' second speech (247c7) – and they should presumably not be discouraged from doing so.

163. *ones you and I made*: So Socrates is still holding Phaedrus jointly responsible for the two speeches he gave.

164. *pair of speeches*: I.e. (what we would call) Socrates' pair of speeches.

165. *someone . . . them*: The point, as it will emerge, is that the first of Socrates' speeches pretended to give an account of the *whole* of *erôs* when in fact only describing an *aspect* of it (i.e. its 'left-handed' aspect).

166. *names of just, or good*: I.e. the names that belong to what is (actually) just and good.

167. *most people*: Or 'the masses' (*to plêthos*).

168. *dear thing*: The Greek is *philê kephalê* (literally 'dear head'), a poetic expression, here presumably used ironically ('dear thing' is perhaps the closest English can get to the same effect, insofar as *kephalê* is essentially a place-filler

169. *ending*: Cf. n. 131 above.

170. *Midas the Phrygian*: The legendary King Midas (eighth century BC).

171. *the speech*: 'The speech' is either Socrates' second speech by itself ('passing over' to praise after the censure of the first), or both speeches together, now treated as one – which they will immediately be in any case (see 265d7; though they are two again in 265e–266b).

172. *two kinds of thing*: I.e. *eidê*: as it turns out, the two sides of a particular kind of *method* ('collection and division').

173. *perceiving together . . . many places*: 'Collection' – probably to be distinguished from, but analogous in structure to, the more basic process of building up universal concepts that Socrates described at 249b–c.

174. *instruct*: 'Instruct', or 'teach' (*didaskein*), will now be the appropriate term, if – as Socrates has argued – the speaker is always to be concerned with the *truth*.

175. *speech*: See n. 171 above.

176. *kind by kind*: I.e. 'kind of thing by kind of thing': *eidos* again. These *eidê* (kinds, forms) will also be Platonic Forms (see n. 101

above). But although Phaedrus had an introduction of sorts to these entities in Socrates' speech (those things like Beauty mysteriously located in the 'region above the heavens'), he is no metaphysician, and the whole context is framed so far as possible in plain speech.

177. *to look to one and to many*: I.e. to collect and divide in the way specified.

178. *in his . . . god*: Adapted from Homer (*Odyssey* 2.402).

179. *And . . . knows*: With these words Socrates comes as close as he can to treating the person in question (the 'dialectician') as if he were a god: 'if I have got your name right' is a typical apologetic formula used in addressing a god – but then 'god (only) knows' makes it clear that he *isn't* in fact divine.

180. *experts in dialectic*: I.e. *dialektikoi*, experts in the science of *dialegesthai*, (philosophical) conversation, where the special nature of the conversation in question is marked by its use of 'collection and division'.

181. *Royal these people are*: For Phaedrus, at least, they perhaps are real kings (of their art)?

182. *the rhetorical . . . us*: So Phaedrus resists Socrates' invitation to assimilate rhetoric, the 'science of speaking', as a whole to dialectic; and Socrates himself will go on to allow that there is rather more to speaking than just grasping, and telling, the truth.

183. *the worthy Theodorus*: Cf. 261c. Socrates goes on to give something of a roll-call of rhetorical experts (most of whom appear as characters elsewhere in Plato); his tone unmistakably suggests the same light irony as his treatment here of Theodorus.

184. *force*: The term (*rhômê*) is the same as the one Socrates used for the definition of *erôs* at 238b–c.

185. *the Chalcedonian*: I.e. Thrasymachus (see 261c, and n. 159 above); Socrates uses a Homeric turn of phrase to refer to someone who was – to judge by his performance in the first book of the *Republic* – a powerful presence.

186. *Acumenus*: See 227a.

187. *Pericles*: The outstanding Athenian statesman and orator (immortalized by the great funeral speech given to him in Thucydides' *History of the Peloponnesian War*) is compared, via a reminiscence of Tyrtaeus, the Spartan poet, to Adrastus, a king of Argos who led the Seven against Thebes.

188. *who . . . converse*: I.e., in light of what has preceded, 'who are ignorant of dialectic'; but it must be open to question whether

Pericles, let alone Adrastus, would have matched up to Socrates' specifications for expertise in dialectic.

189. *babbling and lofty talk*: These are the sorts of things philosophers tend to be described as indulging in by non-philosophers – so, especially, in Aristophanes' *Clouds*, in which Socrates himself is a main character; Socrates in Plato's *Apology* refers to Aristophanes' treatment of him (as meddling with 'things under the earth and in the heavens', 19b); and then in the parable of the ship in the *Republic*, the true steersman, standing in for the philosopher, is said by the ordinary sailors (the people) to be 'a star-gazer' (*meteôroskopos*), a babbler and a good-for-nothing' (*Republic* 488e–489e; cf. *Statesman* 299b). But here in the *Phaedrus*, 'lofty talk', *meteôrologia* (literally, pretty much what the *meteôroskopos* does, i.e. look at *ta meteôra*, 'things on high/ in the heavens'), will surely have special resonance – recalling the heavenly experiences and aspirations of the disembodied soul.

190. *Anaxagoras*: Socrates seems to be punning: the natural philosopher Anaxagoras of Clazomenae, apparently an intimate of Pericles', gave *nous*, 'Mind' or 'Intelligence', a leading role in his account of the coming-into-being of the universe (and in the process talked about what things were like in the beginning, before Mind intervened); what Anaxagoras should have taught Pericles – and what we have no evidence Plato thought he did teach him – is the difference between intelligent *thinking* and the lack of it.

191. *by knack and experience*: Cf. 260e5.

192. *by applying . . . words*: 'Medicines' translates *pharmaka*, 'excellence' is *aretê* (traditionally translated as 'virtue'), 'words' are *logoi* (of course). The redefinition of rhetoric continues apace: no Lysias, no Gorgias could have compared it to medicine, a science of *improving souls* (minds).

193. *the whole*: The whole universe, or the whole soul? Socrates leaves it open: in the context of what follows, it ought to be the latter, but in light of what has *just* been said (about the need for 'lofty talk'), it could still be the former.

194. *Hippocrates the Asclepiad*: Asclepius was the mythical founder of medicine (of the physicians' guild, as it were), Hippocrates the medical writer *par excellence*: medical opinion could come no higher.

195. *argument*: So *argument* (*logos* yet again) is what matters, not (mere) authority.

196. *forms*: Another non-technical use of *eidos* (see n. 176 above);

'complex', just above, is, more literally, 'many-formed', *polueides*.

197. *kinds*: The word is *genos*, as it happens, but it might just as well have been *eidos*.

198. *model speech*: Lysias' speech at the beginning of the *Phaedrus* is one such, given for display.

199. *not on this one*: I.e. rhetoric.

200. *how one should write*: I.e. (as the immediate sequel shows) in a rhetorical handbook.

201. *to borrow his name from*: Socrates is probably making fun here of Tisias' teacher Corax, whose name means 'Crow'.

202. *things*: Or (if we were still in the context of Socrates' second speech) 'the things that are': *ta onta*.

203. *gratifying*: The verb is the same as in the original 'favours should be granted to a man who is not in love . . .' at 227c7–8.

204. *of noble stock*: Compare 246a7–8: 'Now in the case of gods, horses and charioteers are all both good themselves and of good stock . . .'; surely a deliberate reminiscence. Similarly, 'the way round' (*periodos*), in the next sentence, must surely be meant to recall that other *periodos*, the soul's circuit of the heavens (247d5).

205. *Yet . . . others*: What this seems to mean is that ordinary, every-day goals can best be achieved by acquiring knowledge first; but where has this been argued for? Should we perhaps see here a covert reference to the goals of the lover (and of Lysias' supposed non-lover), combined with the description in Socrates' second speech of the pair who fall just short of the ideal – because they give in to their black horses, and have sex?

206. *the beautiful*: Neuter or masculine (plural)? Again, the Greek leaves it open.

207. *writing*: It may look as if we are turning from speaking to writing; in fact, as soon becomes clear, we are turning from the subject of what is scientific or not in *logoi* (spoken or written) to what is appropriate or not in *logoi* (spoken or written).

208. *conjectures*: I.e. *doxasmata*; the word is closely related to *doxa*, 'opinion', on which see n. 105 above.

209. *elixir*: *Pharmakon*.

210. *they are . . . themselves*: The verb for 'reminding' here, *anami-mnêiskesthai*, corresponds to the noun *anamnêsis*, translated as 'recollection' at 249c2.

211. *oak and rock*: I.e. to *any* source ('oak or rock' is proverbial; see e.g. Homer, *Odyssey* 19.162–3 – which may actually be in Plato's mind here).

212. *another kind of speech*: I.e. another kind of speaking (*logos*).
213. *animate*: I.e. 'ensouled' (*empsuchon*).
214. *garden of Adonis*: Plants would be forced in pots during the festival of Adonis.
215. *pieces of knowledge*: I.e., as I have taken it, bits of knowledge about the important subjects in question (the Greek has just the plural of *epistêmê*, 'knowledge'). However, Terry Penner has almost succeeded in persuading me that Socrates means, or might mean, just plural 'knowledges': knowledge of the just, knowledge of the beautiful (or fine), knowledge of the good. In that case the reference here would be to the ideal, expert knower, corresponding to the expert farmer – and specifically not to the mere dialectician, who at least by implication will be denied the title of 'wise' or knowing (279d).
216. *beautiful*: Or 'fine' (noble): the Greek word is *kalos*, which covers both – and for Socrates/Plato, the fine *is* the beautiful.
217. *reaches ... age*: Probably a quotation, from an unknown poetic source.
218. *if someone ... speak of*: Phaedrus here picks up on Socrates' idea of writing for amusement, stories being the obvious example. But there is perhaps also a covert reference, on Plato's part, either to Socrates' second speech (which, of course, Plato *wrote*) or to the defence of justice in the *Republic*.
219. *complex*: 'Complex' is now *poikilos*, 'many-coloured', 'variegated'.
220. *rhapsodes*: Professional performers of poetry (Ion, in Plato's *Ion*, is one).
221. *discourses*: Another rendering of *logoi* (I tried 'speeches' again here in the original version of the present translation, but that no longer seems helpful to me).
222. *arguments*: Or (and) 'speeches' (*logoi* again). Perhaps 'things said' would be enough.
223. *of little worth*: Or even 'of no worth' – that is, by comparison with what he has to say *now*, on revisiting the same subject.
224. *philosopher*: I.e. again, a lover of wisdom (*philo-sophos*).
225. *Isocrates*: A brilliant rhetorician, teacher and speech-writer of Plato's own generation, who also wrote against Plato – and who would no longer have been young by the time of writing of the *Phaedrus*. This is something we need to bear in mind when reading what Socrates goes on to say about him: whether or not he went on to 'greater things', from Plato's point of view, must be open to question, at least insofar as it is certain that he never

became a *dialectician* of the sort Socrates has described in the *Phaedrus* (and would have been appalled at the suggestion that he should).

226. *desires*: I.e. the *sôphrôn*, the self-controlled, restrained person. (For gold: cf. 235d–e.)

THE STORY OF PENGUIN CLASSICS

Before 1946 ...'Classics' are mainly the domain of academics and students, without readable editions for everyone else. This all changes when a little-known classicist, E. V. Rieu, presents Penguin founder Allen Lane with the translation of Homer's *Odyssey* that he has been working on and reading to his wife Nelly in his spare time.

1946 *The Odyssey* becomes the first Penguin Classic published, and promptly sells three million copies. Suddenly, classic books are no longer for the privileged few.

1950s Rieu, now series editor, turns to professional writers for the best modern, readable translations, including Dorothy L. Sayers's *Inferno* and Robert Graves's *The Twelve Caesars*, which revives the salacious original.

1960s The Classics are given the distinctive black jackets that have remained a constant throughout the series's various looks. Rieu retires in 1964, hailing the Penguin Classics list as 'the greatest educative force of the 20th century'.

1970s A new generation of translators arrives to swell the Penguin Classics ranks, and the list grows to encompass more philosophy, religion, science, history and politics.

1980s The Penguin American Library joins the Classics stable, with titles such as *The Last of the Mohicans* safeguarded. Penguin Classics now offers the most comprehensive library of world literature available.

1990s The launch of Penguin Audiobooks brings the classics to a listening audience for the first time, and in 1999 the launch of the Penguin Classics website takes them online to a larger global readership than ever before.

The 21st Century Penguin Classics are rejacketed for the first time in nearly twenty years. This world famous series now consists of more than 1300 titles, making the widest range of the best books ever written available to millions – and constantly redefining the meaning of what makes a 'classic'.

The Odyssey continues ...

The best books ever written

PENGUIN CLASSICS

SINCE 1946

Find out more at www.penguinclassics.com